THE WORLD'S PROBLEMS AND SOLUTIONS:
DIVERSITY ISSUES ANALYSIS

THE WORLD'S PROBLEMS AND SOLUTIONS:
DIVERSITY ISSUES ANALYSIS

DEALING WITH HUMAN RACE, HUMAN
RIGHTS, PHILOSOPHY, SCIENTIFIC, RELIGIOUS,
AND WORLD ECONOMIC ISSUES

LEON KABASELE

authorHOUSE®

AuthorHouse™ UK Ltd.
1663 Liberty Drive
Bloomington, IN 47403 USA
www.authorhouse.co.uk
Phone: 0800.197.4150

Published by AuthorHouse 04/09/2014

ISBN: 978-1-4969-7771-7 (sc)
ISBN: 978-1-4969-7772-4 (e)

Library of Congress Control Number: 2014906844

CONTENTS

PREFACE

When I started to think of the world's problems, I said to myself, "There cannot be the poor without the rich." I began to go in-death about the problems in the world. I believe that when you are looking for solutions, another problem will rise up. The consciousness of many people started to change because they started to do something which they'd never done before in their lives. I realised that the world requires diverse solutions. I started looking for the main solutions before seeking the problems; this means that everything must be possible, because human beings are more valuable than other things. I have been thinking how the world has been affected, the cause of the affection, and how the world can come up with the solution to solve the problem.

I realised that when there was financial crisis in 2007-2008, many authors wrote books about the financial crisis; they published the books in the same year and failed to mention many points which were not realised because they were in hurry to write. I call this missed information because when you are analysing for something that just happened, it is always called a draft or a rough analysis, because later you will come back to correct your analysis. When I took my time, after about six years I began to see the causes of the financial crisis. In this book I identify many issues, especially philosophy and scientific issues which affect many different types of crises in human society.

When I was doing the research to write this book, I discovered many problems in the world to which people do not pay intention, but they are very important for the human being to consider. Most readers will love this book because they will consider many truth histories that took place in the world. Those truth histories, which I analyse in this book, touched me, and I felt that everybody needs the solution of her or his own problem. In this book I develop the processes philosophies of the problems: how can the problem of politics be resolved? Everybody needs to have the right to express her or his opinion for the development of her or his country, and it should be better when the freedom given to citizens includes their right of expression.

INTRODUCTION

Solutions are very important to everybody. Each individual needs a solution, as does each family, each countr, and each continent. All worlds require solutions to the problems people are facing. Since the creation of the world, there have always been problems. A human being cannot live without a problem; even a little baby who has just come out of her mother's womb has her own problem, and that problem requires also a solution.

This book identified many issues concerning the world's solution, as well as where the world's problem is coming from, because there is always a solution to any problem. There is not a solution without a problem, and there is no problem without a solution; both system and method always come together. The world was not made to be empty; if the world was supposed to be empty, there would not be any problems in the world. Of course God made this planet be filled not only with human beings but all types of creatures to compose the world. There were also the equations to put everything together; after that, there was a solution. In the Jews' philosophy, after the problem there was the solution, and God felt good (Gen. 1:31). There was a peace in Godhead, but what about the living the creatures which were created? They also to look for their own peace (Matt. 10:34). Human beings need to look for their own food in their own ways, without asking for God to give them foods forever without going to work. If the world was made that way, everybody should not need to look for the solution, because the solution itself should come automatically. Since the beginning there have always been struggles to become good; this is one of the issues to discuss about the human race and the different races.

The world's problem is also based on many areas of our lives, because we are living in human societies and there are always problems within humans. There is no need to escape from world problems; I believe that more people are running from their problems, and so more problems are coming to them. But rather than searching for the cause of the problems, I am going to develop many different issues in these books to help humanity understand the idea of world problem solving. We cannot live in the world without searching for the cause of the problems and giving the solutions to those problems to future generation so that they may benefit. Realising what is going on in our precious world can help us to live abundantly in this world. God gave us this world for a good purpose, and some of the biggest purposes are to take care of the world in good ways, and to love one other in order to fulfil our satisfactions.

Every human being has a dignity to live in her life according to her own morality; God gave mankind the liberty to live in freedom without any bad condition. From Christianity's perceptive, a human being is set free from God. Islam believes that everything the human being does comes from God. Hinduism believes that there is no word for sin. In these three different beliefs, what they called Abrahamic Religion, there is always something that can tell us about freedom. As I mentioned before, humans were created for a purpose, but it has been dangerous. Most people are very ignorant, and this means there is a way for the solution, but many people think to find that solution for themselves.

The problem of the world is to consider that the world is not an empty planet. One must take into consideration that everything on the planet is very useful and valuable. Even in one particular place, country, or continent, the aspect of life is very important. When every existence lives in this world, it is always welcome in the presence of every creature. People in the world also have their own ways of thinking in order to communicate with each other, both spiritually and physically. When people start to recognise their languages—not the tribes' languages but the direct communication from one other—this will be one of the biggest challenges in human society. If you want to change a human being's mind, you need to speak the person's particular language. I learned this when I was studying for my BSc in computer networks: some of my colleagues were begging me to help them by explaining the coursework to them. In that period I was studying Java and C++ programming. When I explained to them about the coursework, some of them said that I was speaking their language, and this meant that I was explaining to them directly. One of the reasons was because I knew their countries' backgrounds, their responsibilities, and why they were studying for that course. I had to go back consciously with the physical explanation for them to understand their work; I had to use visible materials such as fruits and instruments.

Today the world tries very hard to uncover the biggest organisations which are in the world. I think it is hard to separate salt from sugar, but to God it is very possible and simple to do the separation. The conception of humanism is that every human society is in the form of a tree, because we are all from the same roots in terms of spiritually. The spirit does not die. There is always something that tells us consciously there is only one spirit but different bodies. When you look at a tree, you can see all the branches are separated in different direction, but they have the same roots. I cannot say that a tree has the same fruits, because I was surprised to see a tree with different fruits in the Democratic Republic of the Congo. Generally we say that we will recognise a tree by its fruit; let us agree with this ideology to keep it simple. If each individual person understands that everyone is very important in this world, there is transparency, and each individual should be considered equally. When today's world problem cannot be resolved, one of the reasons is that there are groups in this world that are playing egoism by not considering other organisations. Most of the biggest organisations believe that perhaps because they are the biggest by occupying other organisations, and they think they can impose on them by telling them what to do. This is one of the mistakes in this world, because the biggest organisations are very ignorant. The word is ignorant rather than foolish because in my research and analysis,

I saw that without the small organisations, the biggest organisations would not exist. For instance, there cannot be a country without population, they cannot be a president without population to vote for him, and there cannot be a student without a teacher—or a teacher without a student. The question will always be, who do you lead or what instruction do you follow?

The privilege of the world's solution is not necessary to look at the biggest parts. Those biggest are not too sure about themselves regarding the world's solution, because they are always in front of the smallest organisations. This is a time for those who think that they are bigger than others to draw back and consider the smaller groups. This is why the car manufacturers always design their vehicles with mirrors to look back, to the front, and to the sides: they want it to have a big vision. One of the philosophical reasons is to consider even the pedestrians, because in many countries human rights are not respected, and people do not consider the pedestrians. In many countries, people who drive consider all pedestrians as poor people. I sometimes walk to see what the drivers would think of me when I am crossing the streets. One day a driver insulted me and asked why I was crossing the road slowly. I always felt happy because I was watching the drivers, and I knew that those countries did not respect human beings; they judged all pedestrians.

I believe everything has an opposition, and one system or idea cannot be positive without a negative conception. As I always say, there wouldn't be live without death; live comes from death, and death comes from live. Every human being is aimed to be born and then to die. There is rebirth, but the body should be destroyed before it takes place. If there was a rebirth automatically, there would be a choice before being born, and I believe all would prefer to be born and reborn in the royal families. Imagine the amount of people who are suffering around the world physically and spiritually. Nobody would be reborn outside of the royal families.

In this book, I will introduce you into the topic of the human race. According to my research, there is not just one human race on the planet. The human race is one of the methods that we use to group a certain category of people. Within the human race, many things can be found that are very useful for the solution of the world, because the world needs solutions to the many problems that come to all races of the people on earth. After analysing the human races, the populations should also recognise their own problems. When people think of the ethnic groups in the world, that ideology will help us to understand the solutions within each ethnic group. The ethnic groups have many problems in society; that is a part of the main issues used to raise the problems. There are many cultures in each country and continent; the cultures are also the groups that can have a diversity problem, because those groups always have different people with different ideas. Generally thinking, every human being belongs to one class, which is Homo sapiens. In this general thinking for categorising a human being, in this book I will discuss the scientific organisation for suggesting the human race's scientific and philosophical ideology. The source of each country is within the same country, with people who share the same mentalities. If this is the case, I think it would not have an opposition party, because everybody should think the same. When there is opposition, this means that even within the background of that country, those ethnics groups are coming from the same country. The problem can rise up psychologically due to the different ethnic backgrounds. I have watched documentaries about the original DNA for the United Kingdom, France, Belgium, Spain, and more. Of the people who live there now, most of them do not have origins from that particular place.

Every human being has the right to live according to what he wants to contribute to the nation, because everybody has five senses, and every human being does not think like an animal. A good lawyer listens to her client's argument or story, and afterwards she debates to the court using the argument of that story. In this book I will discuss in detail human rights, but in different ways, because I have already mentioned human rights in one of my book, *Christian Philosophy:*

Understanding Racial Oppression. I will develop the concept and add things I did not mention there, because the more I live, the more I can see the world is changing. I will discuss big organisations that support human rights in the world, especially their advantages and disadvantages. I see there are a lot of conflicts about human rights in different countries; we are going to postulate that if the phrase "human rights" did not exist, what else would happen in the world? Let us think of some of the countries where they think of human rights but do not say it or practise it. I will talk about the UN because it is one of the biggest organisations in the world that is behind human rights. The world needs to think of the intervention of the UN in the particular. One of the base principles that is well-known it is to protect the population, especially when there is rebellion and war in that particular country. The world cannot just find a solution in particular groups or organisations, even if these are the biggest organisations that represent certain countries. However, there are still ways to think outside the box rather than looking at the mechanisms that are already established.

The reason why I included the philosophy of different continents is to find out the basic debate issues in each particular continent. Africa's philosophy is one, and Western philosophy is another. In this book I will discuss and debate the metaphysics and epistemology of Africa. The world solution must also consider the area of Africa because of the size of the continent and its Diaspora.

The European philosophy is the Greek philosophy's, extended and developed further. Europe is from where the philosophy started to be improved around the world, solving many issues on each continent. The Europeans started understanding the problems of the world, and they began to search for other aspects around the world. In this book I will talk about the major reason why the Europeans discovered many continents; this is one of the methods where the problem came from, but it was not a bad idea.

The Asian philosophy introduces the religions on which the majority of Asians rely, and they think the solution will only come from the religions. I also will discuss how Asian philosophy from a religious perspective can help the entire world with its solutions.

The American continent's philosophy started when liberation was considered, as well as the freedom of all the races. It was not just the black colonisation; many other races were also colonised. In this book I will debate the colonisation of the different human races and the development of the US philosophy.

For the Oceania philosophy, I will discuss their cultures, the main issues, and the most common issues within their cultures. I believe that everywhere human beings live, there are always debates because people have their own ways of viewing matters.

The causes of the conflicts in the world come from many different issues. Many of the conflict come from the past; they were never given solutions, and the world still faces the same situations but in different forms. I will discuss the different types of conflicts across these nations. I believe that if we want to find out about the world's solutions, we have to formulate the symptoms of the world's problems: what are the conflicts within these symptoms? In this book, I selected the most important problems and easy ways to know from where the conflicts used to come. I realised that the wars in the past had not finished yet, because they have been transformed into different wars. There is also the interfering of spiritual matters, because in the postcolonial period, many of the Africans gave their totems away, but today there are the conflicts within many African cultures. There are religion conflicts, and many of the religions in the world do not have the same philosophies and religious psychologies. I wrote a book called *African Inter-dialogue Religion: Philosophy and Theology*. The readers will understand how the African religions interact with each other for the development of African religions. If today the religions started to interact with each other, I think it is one of the world solutions.

Another conflict is culture imposing. Many of the problems within the cultures come from external forces. The postcolonials introduced its traditions to other cultures in that period. It is not a bad thing to introduce other cultures in different countries, because when people mature, they will find it very difficult to quickly learn other things. I will come up with many debates about the conflicts around the world—not personal conflicts but in each continent of the world.

The world's economic crisis is also one of the problems in the world. In this matter human beings start looking for a solution, and people often think back to war because they lost money. I called this a war on finances because everything requires money; even the little children feel that their parents cannot afford what they want, but they still survive. The countries across the world are affected due to the financial crisis; the governments are affected, and the department of education starts pushing very hard for the population to return back to study and hard work. This ideology will help governments get money from students. The party politics are affected, and many of the politicians around the world do not respect the rules of politics because of financial matters; each political movement expects the solution for its country will come from financial means. Social life is affected, and the main issue of the social conflict is for the evolution of the country. Every time when there is a conflict within society, if the solution has been given, then the life of the population will be develop. The religions can be affected when the population is consciously unwell. I believe that a high majority of the people in the world belong to a particular religion. If this is the case, then religion is major environment for world problem—solving, especially when real religion is an institution that helps the world. This is a book that can contribute to the world solution.

I worked very hard spiritually and physically to understand the world's problems. The world economic crisis is not just the major area of the world problem; it is an area where most human beings focus because most of the solutions require finances.

SECTION 1

Human Race: Problem and Solution

The original human beings that lived before us still live, because they can be still identified all over the world. The species still lives on earth because every creature needs social life, and this means that when there is human being productivity, any existence on earth requires social life. Mosley argued that "huge debates rage about human origins, but the broad consensus among scientists is that all the different species of human that have ever existed were descended from ape-like creatures that walked upright in Africa more than six million years ago. These creatures had many descendants, most of which became extinct, but the first creature we would recognise as human first appeared in Africa two million years ago" (Mosley, 2011, *BBC News*). There is no need to stop productivity; there will be always problems when there is a reduction of productivity. Every creature has a right to live with dignity according to what he wants to do on earth. A long time ago, when I was doing my master class, they decided to reduce the number of students in the class due to a lack of space. The programme manager came up with the idea to keep those who were catechism. One of the students said, "What about the pure catechism student?" But that teacher didn't have a response that was convenient. I was not catechism, and I received an e-mail that said my application was declined, but they never told me a reason. From the beginning of everything, the development of human beings cannot be stopped; our population is growing, more problems are appearing, and more struggles are taking place to resolve certain problems on earth. It has been said that "According to Professor Chris Stringer of the Natural History Museum in London, fossil evidence is increasingly suggesting that human evolution followed the same pattern . . . 'only one of which, an ancestor of our species, was ultimately successful in evolutionary terms,' he said. According to Dr Leakey, the growing body of evidence to suggest that humans evolved in the same way as other animals shows that 'evolution really does work'." (Ghosh, 2013, *BBC News*). There will always be problems, even if we try to reduce the population around the world, because humanity cannot be stopped from growing, and nobody would accept being eliminated in order for another person to replace him.

The problem will never end as long as the solution is never taken, because of the productivity of the new generation. Until now there are only two different types of humanisms. The ancestral was showed non-developing human beings; I believe that they do not have a good development of information technology, but they have knowledge to resolve their problems with help. In this latest generation, where there is a high development of information technology, human beings still struggle to find solutions in certain things; every human being requires development, but the solution becomes very tough. The governments start thinking even to get more money, and the money must come from the small, poor families. I saw this situation in one of Africa's countries: there was discussion about the world crisis because there was not enough information for the population to understand the crisis. The government of that poor country changed the population to pay the expensive taxes, and everybody started to complain. I was very surprised to see people live in the twenty-first century still having problems with getting world information, so I qualified this as bad governance because they could not give the world information to their population. These sorts of the problems must be resolved. A human being has the right to get the information. This is not the problem of feeding the population, but it is about the communication of the entire population in that particular country. In today's world, human beings have become very lazy, and one of the reasons is that in the past, human beings were very strong because Homo sapiens lived in the tropics or mountains in certain parts of the world.

I would like to introduce research that made many organisations update their previous research about discovering the skull. It has been said that "In Georgia, researchers have found a skull 1.8 million years old. A discovery that calls into question the entire history of human evolution because it suggests that the hominids of the time, whether in Europe or in Africa, belonged to a single species. And if researchers were misled about the evolution of the human species? Surprising as it may seem, this is indeed suggests a new study by Swiss researchers and Georgians in the journal Science. The origin of this work: a skull 1.8 million years old discovered in Georgia, in a village called Dmanisi. It is one of the oldest sites known to have been populated by ancestors of the man once they out of Africa" (*Gentside Découvertes,* 18 October 2013). As I stated before, part of this development in the species Homo sapiens is that they do not just live in the tropics only, but they represent the ancestors of all mankind. People should know that they are not just from their parents' biology—their parents also had parents, and so on. We are from them not just because of their appearances, and even their skulls can still remind us this is a real human being like us. The world changes. The moon, sun, stars, and other living creatures still look the same, but none of the scientists are thinking to change them. I believe if archaeology keeps digging, there will be more skulls that are more than what they've already discovered, and many people will again be surprised. I remember that in the past, one doctor discovered another part of human beings. People might say that we have arms, legs, and heads, so why do we need one more part in our bodies, and to do what? The reason is that another sickness might arise in somebody else, and perhaps that symptom will be caused by that new part of the body. I believe that there are many things that have not been discovered on this planet. Every day the new things must come up in order to help the existence of human beings.

I introduced this paragraph not only because of the debate concerning the discovery of another skull, but because others that will be discovered. There is no need to be confused by new things because there still are more things to come which we have not had the opportunity to know. The problems that can arise must come from former archaeology, and new archaeological digs will discover them because they did not discover the same skulls at the same times. The debates here are to think of the result of the research, some which will take place because of the skills and experiences of the archaeologists that dig. If we look at in the past, we might consider that they were not the materials that could clearly show the exact environment when the skulls were found. On the other hand, the new archaeologists have the opportunities because the digging materials have been developed, and they can show most of the exact environment. Perhaps the old archaeology had computer technology to detect the bones, as well as other necessary things, and now they are using camera recorders that can film the movements or events in the place where they are working. There was no opportunity for the old archaeologists to do this work because most of them were using poor equipment, and there was no choice because of a lack of technology. There is no need to suggest that there is confusion; I believe that in the future, there will be another skull discovered, and people will analyse in the same manner. One of the solution for the debate is to understand the old archaeologists' equipment used in that period, compare it to now, and update the equipment in order to discover more skulls. Human beings cannot live with the same materials over and over; if mankind does not develop, there is no point to the productivity.

Race is a concept that distinguishes all types of human beings. We can see the difference ourselves when we look at each other. If somebody sees a black person, automatically the viewer person will think of Africa. When somebody sees a white or fair person, he will think of Western world. The same reflex occurs with an Asian person. There is no need to stop somebody from judging, though many people say that when you identify, it means that you judge somebody negatively. You cannot stop somebody from seeing, judging, or identifying. If you keep stopping people from doing what is natural for a human being to do, it means that you are pushing yourself very hard to become the world's police officer. As long as a human being was made to give the difference of something, let it go. Perhaps you yourself do it at all the time but do not realise it.

The good things of this distinction are also to recognise the population in this planet; everybody should belong to a particular group of people. Human beings are divided into many race groups, as well; as being divided geographically; where a particular group of people lives, there must be a country. People in that particular continent often have the same manner of thinking, and there will be the same race as a majority. However, there will not be the same language because of subgroups, known as countries. A country always comes after the principles of the continent, because the continent resembles the major species, and one of the biggest is Homo sapiens. Religion is also part of the system that can categorise a group of human beings, because philosophy states that everybody wants to discover the power which is more than her imagination; this is why religion is a part of groups and allows people to express their feelings.

Most of the problems used to come from the religious groups that did not have the same philosophies. When the people arise from the religions, the solution will never come from the government—the solution can only come when the heads of the religious organisations agree with what they are doing; it will always be spiritually first before it manifests physically. Every religion has its own problem within them. When the Catholic Church stated that priests could not get married or even have children, some of the priests left Catholicism to join the Anglican Christianity denomination, because the Anglicans let their priests wed and have children. I had a word with one of the theologian doctors in one of my classes, and he said that everything started getting better because the Catholic Church was trying to change certain rules, and this ideology would bring part of the solution. I do not suggest the Catholic Church will change its mind because of the Anglicans—if it changes because of that, it means it acted foolishly. It must change because of the priests are also human beings. God created sex with a purpose, and that purpose was not for pleasure but for human being's productivity.

As human beings, communication is very important, and to change human beings' minds, one must teach them a new language so that their minds might change. When I came to London, I had a problem because of the English language. Without a language there cannot be communication. I believe that every human being needs to live with people with whom he can communicate properly. Communication is always good to people. People say that Homo sapiens live somewhere in Africa, Asian, and America, but I realise this is one of the problems in our society. This rejects another part of the human beings in the planet; some of the scientists qualify them as monkeys. I believe that to eat a monkey is a taboo, but it is in Asian religions, as well as in Europe. I also saw people eat monkey in Africa, and those who eat monkey will contradict this ideology.

When people are together, there is always a composition of the cultures, because human beings are productive, and multiple families create different mind-sets. Everybody will not have the same thinking or ideology. In the beginning of the creation of human beings, there was always struggle in all areas of life. I believe that due to a lack of medicine knowledge, many people were buried alive. The struggles of the productivity of the human being never ended—in fact it is still multiplying now. Humans are still developing, and there is nothing that can stop it. There have been two world wars in the past, and many people died, but these wars never stopped the productivity of human beings. In cultures, there is always nationalism that can distinguish the citizens of a particular country, and they have also their principles. A problem can occur when there is another challenge from a different culture. In the postcolonial and missionaries period, there was many problems because the original people's cultures were starting to mix up with the new ones. Many cultures around the world today have difficulty returning to the principles of their original cultures, because they are already used to new cultural influences that the missionaries and post-colonials brought to them. Many marriages have been changed; the original people cannot follow their original principles, and this is one of the problems divorces use to justify quitting, resulting in many single parents. One of the reasons to resolve divorce is to look back from the original principles of the culture, and to respect the marriage in order to function very well.

Somebody called me on Skype and asked me a question. There was a problem in his African country: somebody was married to a wife, but the wife was married to another person in the council (court justice) via a signed document. When the problem came up, the justice of that country decided to give that woman to the man who went in the council, and the second man who married her lost his wife.

The population can be identified from their different ancestral roots. Some of the ancestors left principles for their next generation to follow. Ethnicity is one ideology that can help human beings to be in groups with the same ancestry. A family is not just a father, a mother, and the children, but every family that came before. There are also links that are still performed within each family. Especially in ethnic groups that authorise polygamy, one might see family members marring each other without realising it, and this situation is causing many problems. The problems will arise to destroy the family. Even in the past, people from the same family were marrying each other, and the ideology was about the productivity of mankind. However, when the numbers of the world populations are sufficient, there is no need for those kinds of things. Nobody will tolerate having the pleasure to produce children with one's own mother or father. Some people used to do that, and the primary reason is based on ancestral philosophy; they used to do that without embarrassment. Many families split because of these situations; probably the mother or father does not understand how to deal with this situation, and sometimes suicide might take place. One day, a woman sent me a message on Facebook telling me that her husband had sex with her teenage daughter, and she wanted her husband to die. Many ethnic groups are not destroyed due to the financial crisis, but due to sexual abuses. If the world today does not want to look for these situations, then how can the solution be found?

The solution is something that can bring peace to the ethnic group, because every human being belongs to a particular ethnic group, and that group was made of ancestors who left their principles for the next generation. Modern generations should think about going back and viewing those old principles.

Perhaps after this generation, there will be again another new generation that will come. The method of this world is functioning, and humanism has already understood that after very careful consideration. The world did not face the strategies since the beginning. One of the reasons is that the population was not enough for the problems to arise: many people did not think of banks and other things in the world. According to the fossil skull that has been found, there is always the question of how our ancient ancestors lived. One of the answers could be in that period, social life was not developed in terms of technology, but they had peace of mind. Some of the symptoms were not developed because everybody was living without laws. Today the Homo sapiens that live in the tropics live without governments and laws, but they respect and do not interfere in the humans' social lives. The problems that rise today are always financial because many people do not think there is a need to think of finances immediately after being married.

This typical ideology did not take place in the past. I saw scientists inspecting one of the ancient skulls with many scientific materials, but I do not think that skull told them about difficulties after marriage in the past. There is no need for this generation to think about how their ancestors were living, but they might follow certain principles to compare them with this modern time. A long time ago my mum told me that certain clothes styles which people use now came from the nineteenth century. When I think of the problems of the human race, I believe that there is a huge separation in this generation. Most of the problem is in ignoring others, so this modern time should consider analysing the lives of early people who lived in the past.

SECTION 2

Human Rights: Problem and Solution

Many justices in this world today are about clarifying many issues, including the traditional cultures of different types of people. Also, personal issues are taken into consideration. If the world starts thinking of the justice of considering every human being as an equal, they will not hate another person, and most of those people will contribute to many societies.

Justice has a major role to play in the world today because human beings cannot live without certain conditions. Justice is viewed as a helper in the eyes of the poor, and most of the poor seek help in order to be considered human beings created by God. In a country where human rights are not respected, a rich person raped a young lady in a poor family. When the family went for justice, the rich person paid money, and the justice of that country let him go. The poor family asked for help from the justice, but the justice did not hear their voices. There is no freedom of speech in the most of the countries in the world. In another land, there was a black teenage boy who was stabbed by a white person. A friend of that black teenager ran to tell the police, but the police officer rejected that case and never helped the boy. After the death of the boy, the policeman went to the court to confirm that he knew that case, but he turned down the boy who came to seek help. A black person stabbed a white person, and that black person was put into prison, and then he was killed in prison. These cases show that the world's justice does not help. Human rights are spoken rather than acted, and many civilians in the world seek justice but cannot find it. The justice of the court could give a valuable decision in all those cases. These cases failed, but if the world is functioning with the right justice, I think all those cases would end up with respect towards human beings.

The laws have not protected their principles in the appropriate manner. When we think of the justice, automatically there is a trust of good assurance in our lives, and every human being deserves to be protected from the right law. Also, the major problem for human beings is to protect their precious things, and the law should react as human beings need it to, because the laws were made to treat every human being equally. In these cases, everybody should think that the laws have not been respected. Today the problem arises because the laws are not respected; it is not just about the financial problem in the world, but it is also the fact that justice is not working. Human rights are speaking but are not reacting. The world has urgent requests for human rights, but human beings are not living in a democracy and are asking why they imposed the system of democracy, because this system brought the world violence. Many opposition leaders do not understand what to do in their societies. If the law exists, those who break it should be dealt with in a way to satisfy everybody. As long as somebody lives on earth, more problems will develop because more relationships and more problems arise. When the same person confronts the same situation in the days to come, there is no way for him to go see the justice with trust, because of the experiences he faced in the pass. If a justice does a good job, there will not be any trouble or fear in people's hearts. This situation shows that the world is taken hostage by the bad reaction of the law. Human rights should react in terms of working righteously.

Martin Luther King Jr said, "I have a dream that my four little children will one day live in a nation where they will not be judged by the colour of their skin, but by the sort of persons they are. I have a dream that one day . . . all God's children, black, white, Jews and Gentiles, Protestants and Catholics, will be able to join hands and sing in the words of the black people's old song, Free at last, free at last, thank God Almighty, we are free at last!" (Jenkinks, 2002: 119). King had a hard life, but he never reacted badly because he was after the world's freedom; he understood that every human has a right to live on earth as God wants him to, and there is no need to think of human beings as bad creatures. The world has no respect for humanity. If the world respects human beings, there would not be people such as Martin Luther King, because when somebody complains or demands that something be done, that means there is injustice is going on in that sector. Justice is for everybody; it does not have a colour or race, and so everybody should have a right to it. Children often have no right to express themselves because many people believe that they cannot open their mouths to defend themselves, but they have the major role to play in our societies today. When Martin Luther King talked about the children, he knew that the children need to be respected in the world because they are tomorrow's future. The children will do in the future what we are doing today; we are doing what our parents left us, because every human being comes from one generation and gives to another one. If the last generation did not respect the justice, then the new generation will be the same, and the generation to come will copy them because human beings are all about productivity.

Martin Luther King came with a good ideology and knowledge from God. He was also encouraged by the philosophies of Gandhi, and after analysing all those ideas, he understood humanity. *"Martin Luther King was a Christian and a Baptist minister. He believed that the only way to achieve quality was by non-violent and peaceful forms of protest"* *(Jenkins, 2002: 119)*. Everybody uses his knowledge and emotions in order for the world to be stable. Where there is bad justice, there is also a good justice, because everybody does not think the same way, and there are always challenges where there are the different types of cultures on earth. This earth does not have one culture; if there was only one culture in the world, then the justice would be different, and people would obey one principle. Many people in the world refuse to analyse the visions of others. There are always different religions and cultures that block people from learning new ways. While people start to reject others' knowledge, this will always be a problem. It causes dictators to rise, because people want to remain stable with their ideas and do not to consider other people's knowledge. Knowledge is for everybody. As long as you are living on earth, you will still need other people to help you; you cannot be unique with your own idea and without having any mistakes in your knowledge.

Another aspect of human rights is that every country has the right to contribute their ideas in every situation, and that the world belongs to everybody. The justice is respected not just in particular countries but for every creature without any corruption, and people need to live confidentially with that good justice. Where there is no good justice, there will not be protection from others because people have the right to express themselves in situations. When the populations do not have the opportunity to express their rights in a particular county, that country will always have trouble. The governments in this world, as well as the party politics, have duties to let their populations express their feelings in order to bring peace to the countries.

The deaths of populations occur when the human rights in a country are not respected, and human being has the opportunity to survive. It has been said that "if a woman commits any offence, her penalty is no less or more that a man could expect in a similar case. If she is wronged or harmed, she gets due compensations equal to what a man in her position would get" (Jenkins, 2002: 116). In many countries where feminism method is not taken into consideration—especially in the countries where there is polygamy—they have the right to live in the same house without quarrelling. Women are not considered in many countries for different reasons; in some countries it's because of the religion, and in others it's due to polygamy. I believe that when a woman is not respected in a particular country, there might be injustice against women and children. When certain laws do not respect the personality of females, there is no need to consider that law because it does not have a human race or gender. When the law starts considering certain human races or a certain gender, this law is malfunctioning. We are living in a world where every human being is equal to one another, because we are the same but different in our physical bodies; we are born and we die. If human rights should be authorised, the feminism right is equal to the masculine, and the entire world will be improved. The problem here is that when a woman comes from a country where they do not respect females, or justice does not consider them, she is always eager to live in the countries where she has the right to live like everybody else. Her character might change because she will be influenced by the new system. There was a man who went to marry a wife in a country where there is strong polygamy. When that man decided to bring a wife to London, where the female is more respected than a man, that woman kicked out her husband that brought her to London when he husband wanted to complain, and she called the police. The police stopped her husband from seeing her and living in the same house.

Justice should be taken in to consideration in this world because it is an element for people to rely on and feel confident when they confront it. World justice is always automatic in everybody's mind; every human being was born with something that cannot be taken away. Every human being feels free to do something that is right for the individual to feel happy and to understand what he has been doing is good. In the world, every human being cannot have only one justice or a family that imposes its will upon the entire continent. If there are the problems in the world today, one of the sources of the problems used to come from dictators of nations. Because the justice of this world disappointed them, they suggest that when somebody does bad things, everybody will agree with that person, but when somebody does the right thing, everybody will disagree with that person. World justice does not affect humanism because most of the judgement is not correct; many people realise that justice is not considering the poor, women, and children. If the justice does not obey the rules according to the human being's desire, that justice cannot be justified because it is helping only one side of the camp. People love justice, but the justice has its owner in this situation. It is not supposed to have an owner because it belongs to everybody, and people need to see how justice works. When the population in a particular country feels that justice is perfect for everybody, that particular country should be developed, and the population will live the lives that they deserve. Another country cannot impose justice on another country, because everybody has the right to consider the justice that is in her own country and to understand her culture's needs.

Women must stand against injustice in the world. A woman is made equal to a man spiritually. If today a woman is not taken into consideration in the community, there is no point in mentioning the word justice. One of my teachers, a female, said to us that her husband does everything for her. She concluded by saying that her husband cleaned the house, did the washing in the kitchen, shopped, and performed his own job regularly. Everybody was surprised, especially the students brought up from the countries where women do not have a right to tell their husbands to cook or to do housework. It has been said that "Education paved the way towards gender equality in Europe. Women around the world today are at the front line of the struggle not only for their own rights but also for those of their communities. In the midst of these struggles, many of women's human rights defenders are at risk of becoming victims of human rights abuses themselves" (Jenkins, 2002: 115). Many women are defending their own human rights, and some women start defending their rights violently—not because they are violent people but because they want their voices to be heard in their countries. They use violent actions to pass the message. It has been said that "Uroko Onoka, a wealthy Nigerian man and local philanthropist, was allegedly raped by his six wives after returning home from a bar last Tuesday night. Onoja allegedly resisted the attack at first, but was soon overpowered by the six women who coerced him to have sex with each spouse in ascending order of age" *(International Business Time)*. Everybody knows about Nigeria: it is a country where polygamy is taking place, and most of the population is Muslim. In this Muslim country, the voices of women cannot be heard.

Children have a right to raise their voices, but when they try to be heard, nobody will respect their rights. Many countries do not respect children; they do not understand that children are the future and need extra help to develop that future. Humanitarian news and analysis say that "'We must rid the world of landmines,' Glover said in a statement released by the UN. 'They kill innocent people and children, and no weapon should outlast war itself,' he added while on his first trip as a goodwill ambassador for the UN's Children's Fund (UNICEF)" (Danny Gloves). In Africa and many countries in the world, adults consider children as insects; they forget that they were children before they became adults. Many counties abuse children and mistreat them. When they treat the children in a bad manner, what happens when these children grow up? What are they going to do to others? I think if these types of the situations are not mended, then in the future they will be a serious problem. The world needs to understand the rights that everybody has in this world; we all have the same right to survive on this planet, and everybody has a mission in the world. There are also problems when children do not feel comfortable in their own families, countries, or societies, because their skills or gifts will not be developed. Most of the children deserve to be somebody very important in their countries. Nobody should stop another person from feeling good. The world problem is not just in finance—there are many problems that are more important than the financial, but many people do not consider or focus on them.

The children around the world today do not have the right to express themselves with the freedom that comes from their hearts, and even if others teach them about justice, they do not benefit from what they study. If justice in the world was taken into the consideration by the governments of every country, each country would develop in a way that every citizen would be satisfied—but justice is currently useless, and nothing can be improved. There are many reasons that the world is condemning the children, and one of them is to accuse the children without any good reason. *"It looks at the profile of children that are being accused of being witches and at the effects on them, the causes, which are not only cultural and social, but also economic and political, and origins of witchcraft accusations against children"* (UNICEF, 2011). Those children have a good purpose for their own futures, but they lack knowledge, and their own parents throw them into the streets. In my book *African Inter-religious Dialogue: Philosophy and Theology*, I discussed witchcraft as a religion and stated that it should not treat people in bad way. In the Democratic Republic of the Congo, the majority of the children are poorly treated because witchcraft is abusive. Even some of my uncles were rejected because my grandfather from my mum's family had another wife, and she did not like to see my uncles because they were born from a different mother. I believe that she did not want to see the children of another wife in the house, and she created the maxim to say that the children were witchcraft. She caused trouble in the house for my grandfather until he kicked out my uncles. In Africa there is no social service to report those incidents, and they ended up homeless, struggling in their lives and with no money to survive. Then after my granddad died, my uncles started living their own lives with their own possibilities.

SECTION 3

The Different Philosophical Issues on Different Continents

This world consists of five major continents, instead of seven or six. Each continent has its own understanding of tradition and ethnic groups that can categorise them; also, each individual identifies with and belongs in that continent. The metaphysics, epistemology, and aesthetics which always arise in each of the continents and the populations there used to ask themselves many philosophical questions about the development of their continents. The continent cannot be created by itself, without people; there is no country that has no people in it, and everything within a particular continent concerns its human beings.

There were old philosophies that people used to consider in aspects of their lives, and people want to live in that method for their own understanding. The ancient philosophies helped humanity to grow and to move into the new philosophy in modern times, because people can no longer live in the same understanding of philosophy anymore. If technology is developing every second, what can we say about the philosophy? There must also be a different sort of development of the theologies, which need to be developed. The numbers of the population must grow because human beings were created to multiply, and one family must become more than one through its responsible members. Those five different continents were created because of they have the same philosophical understanding of human productivity and social life. When people are separated, it means there are different understandings, and they decided not to live in the same place. The cause of the language is an element that can organise people to be together in the group; that group can also have the types of foods they like. Even the geography is very important to organise the group, because when people gather with the same language, foods, and characters, they have to have their limitations. Those limitations allow them to understand their own origins and where they belong. If somebody crosses a limitation from where she belongs, that person knows that she is in a different geographical area. In the early days people recognised their limitations by geography and language; even now that philosophy is still in use, but it's not as before because the mentality of human beings constantly changes.

Africa continent is the second biggest continent in the world, and there are many sorts of problems there which the rest of the world does not realise, but the African people need solutions to their problems. Many problems used were caused by confronting other situations in their governments and local communities. Most of the Africa philosophy is based on politics; this is a major process where many troubles developed in Africa, and even the Africans themselves struggle with this issue. One of the reasons is because Africa is new to democracy and Western politics. Since the start of the postcolonial period, there has not been much peace in African countries—there is a lot of struggle, and the population cannot find a way out. Many African philosophies are also based on culture: Africa is a continent where each country has several ethnic groups or tribes, and every ethnic tribe has its own principles. There are different types of tribes in Africa, and there is usually no need to follow their governments; marriages respect the cultures rather than the governments' laws. The laws of marriages in Africa have different conditions because of the number of various tribes. When somebody from a tribe marries somebody from a different tribe, there is always a big debate. I was in Paris, and one young lady told me about her marriage with a French man. Her husband came from France, and he was complaining about the marriage. The problem was because the lady's family was asking for dowry. In that period of 2000-2013, the requirements of the African Congolese culture marriage was that a husband must give a coat for her father, two pairs of shoes for both parent, a cloth for her mother, a goat, fifty to one hundred boxes of beer, and two thousand euros or dollars in cash, plus other small things. When the man completed everything, then they could give him their daughter. That French husband was very upset. I asked the same question to one of the pastors from Cameroon, and she said to me it is the same list used in Cameroon and also Nigeria—and sometimes the price is even higher.

Many Africans consider their own philosophies for dealing with their own cultures matters, rather than exploring other views of life; some of them do not think about their future or teaching their children. Bruce B. Janz's report states, "African philosophy deals with metaphysics, epistemology, axiology, and methodology, as well as with the problems and opportunities of intercultural philosophizing, and does so in ways that cover the gamut of the analytic/continental divide in Western philosophy. The best we can hope to do here will be to hit some high points, and direct the reader to more complete introductions for further information."(2008:2). The cultures become the most important aspects of African philosophy because people think they cannot live without the knowledge of their ancestors, and there is no need to seek for advice from other traditions. There is a problematic belief that the solution can only come from one exclusive philosophy, but most Africans would not join another camp in order to solve their problems. Many Africans say that every time an African president goes to Europe or America, he goes to ask for money rather than helping the population of his country. Many schools in Africa study Western philosophy because their ancestors learned it during the colonial period. I had a conversation with one African that believes the African philosophy of death, and that person did not want me to mention the name of God or discuss anything regarding archaeology. I believe that the philosophy is not universal because the Africans themselves do not want that to be developed—they always say that it is the Westerners that want those scientific methodologies. The debate is, what if the Westerners refuse to join their camps? Where will the solution come from, and how they can be developed? Africans believe in a god, but its name is not the same as God because it has a different meaning. I say this because not all of them go to churches, but many of them believe in the philosophies of their ancestors. The world has many problems that need to be resolved because there a diversity in the religions.

Asian philosophy is on a different multicultural level. As the biggest continent in the world, Asia has more population, and the most popular religion is Buddhism. Koller argued that "Historically and culturally, it is preferable to treat the Indian subcontinent as a whole and convenient to label all of these philosophies "Indian," in the sense of culturally belonging to the Indian subcontinent. When we look at the development of Indian philosophy over the last three thousand years, we can distinguish between different periods of development, each with its own distinct characteristics. We can also see an underlying continuity in which certain basic ideas and attitudes are dominant" (2007: 3). There are several understandings because the continent large enough to fit many cultures, and each has almost the same philosophy, but their religions are always slightly different. Their religions are a type of metaphysics that makes them live in the same society even as they expand, but they can be still identified. They have Buddhism, Hinduism, and Asian epistemology, which helps their knowledge expand so that they can be developed. The minds of Asians are adapting their religions' principles; even their governments are always focussed to hear about their religions, and they have a huge trust from where their knowledge is based. The religions in Asian have important roles to play in their societies; it is a continent where many of their laws are confirmed by their religions. In Pakistan, before travelling out of the country, you must be a Muslim first; this is a problem with other religions such as Christianity, and many Christians suffer due to this law. If the government finds the solution for this issue, I think Pakistan will have a breakthrough. I will develop this section later in this book. Everybody is useful and important—there is no need to reject others because of their religion. Those Christians in Pakistan did not choose to be born in Pakistan, and their religion is their own choice.

India is well organised with their philosophy, according to their research, and they are more focussed on finding and solving the problems in India. Koller argues that "the practical character of Indian philosophy is manifested in a variety of ways. The very word darshana, which is usually translated as "philosophy," points to this. Darshana literally means "vision," that is, what is "seen." In its technical sense it means what is seen when ultimate reality is investigated. The seers of India, seeking the solution to life's sufferings, investigated the conditions of suffering and examined the nature of human life and the world in order to find the causes of suffering and the means for its elimination. What they found constituted their darshana, their philosophy of life" (Koller 2012: 12). In the subcontinent of Asia, their philosophies are more considered because they always work hard to find the solution by doing philosophical research, and the people of India believe that the solution of their problems can only come from their research. The Indian philosophy is determined by the suffering in India; the population cannot accept the problems developed in their country without investigating that problem and analysing that problem. It is always better to find out where the problems are coming from before running to the solutions. Most of the problem used to come from the issue between Christians and the other religions. The population of India trusts themselves before trusting others and looking for the solution in another place. The reason why is that the Indian population is more attached to the United Kingdom; one of the reasons is because they were colonised by British, and they still have that story of colonisation in their mind. Even Gandhi, who was a Christian, went to his traditional religion. The philosophy of India is very interesting in terms of its organisation, because they do not give up doing the investigation and looking for solutions for the future of their country. The Indians always analyse the consequences of their philosophy, because they rely on their elders and overseers to resolve their problems. The consequence of the Indian philosophy is to consider the benefit of the Indian population, when the wiser people or overseers are dealing with the problems of the country, and that would lead to a decree of no killing or destroying anything that belongs to people. Philosophically and politically, they look for the solutions of their countries and the continent in appropriate ways.

The Oceania is a continent that consists of water, because every time people think of Oceania, they always realise that there is an existence of water. Even when I was doing my research on Oceania philosophy, I read about the seas and how the habitants of Australia used to live. There is also the importance of social life in Oceania, because where there is an existence of human beings, there will be always different ideas. It has been said that "by this I mean a political theory according to which legitimate power in Makira, especially the power to understand and administer Makiran kastom, must be inborn (not simply acquired), and is thus, according to some, the rightful province of genuine Makirans only. Such a theory can give rise, furthermore, to what I will term a kastom mysticism, the goal of which is similar in some respects to the goal of reunion with divinity conceived of as a higher self, explicit in many religious and philosophical versions of metaphysical monism" (Hviding and Rio, 2011: 1998). The philosophical problem on the Oceania continent is based on social life; one of the reasons is because this continent was colonised by many different organisations. Their social life is different than others; this continent is increasing with people from different countries around the world. In February 2012 the Australia government stated that "the rest of Australia's people are migrants or descendants of migrants who have arrived in Australia from about 200 countries since Great Britain established the first European settlement at Sydney Cove in 1788. In 1945, Australia's population was around 7 million people and was mainly Anglo-Celtic. Since then, more than 6.5 million migrants, including 675 000 refugees, have settled in Australia, significantly broadening its social and cultural profile". The problem will arise from the diversity of multiple cultures; everybody lives according to his cultural requirements, and everybody is expressing his own point of view. Even the English language is globalising and grouping the population together, but the ethnic groups also have the ability to give their own solutions.

When there is not freedom of speech in a continent or country, people are not comfortable to develop, and that country is likely led by a dictator. It is very important for cultures to be able to share their opinions, because then they will have the ability to develop. In February 2012, the Australia government stated that "the defining feature of today's Australia is not only the cultural diversity of its people, but the extent to which they are united by an overriding and unifying commitment to Australia. Within the framework of Australia's laws, all Australians have the right to express their culture and beliefs and to participate freely in Australia's national life". Everybody has the right to do what others are doing; even if finances are stopping them, the important point is to have human rights and freedom of speech in every land. When cultures have freedom, the religions will have the liberty to develop to help their own countries and continents. When a country is developing, it means that the continent is also developing. Human rights are not just for Australia only but also for the immigrants who live in Australia; they should benefit from human rights and have the liberty to express their own cultures. It is always difficult for every human being to change the culture in a mature age. In hypothetical imperatives, when somebody does something because of the law, the culture says to respect it. You should not do something simply because the law says so; it is better that your morals convince you that it is wrong or right to do, and this will make you feel good. I believe that even if there is a problem in Australia, that problem will involve everybody that lives in Australia, and the solution will arrive from many places and from every culture that is located in Australia.

The American continent is known as a new world in terms of discovering ideas; this is an example of a mixed races continent, where there is a diversity of cultures. This continent has the opportunity to show the world the best example of how cultures can survive together. The American philosophy is based on Aristotle, because he was the basis for the development of the consequence issue, but Emmanuel Kant came after him with the development of the moral issue. Everything in philosophy should acknowledge the philosophy of Aristotle or Emmanuel Kant, and everybody must follow it. The advantage of the philosophy in America is because they develop, and based on that philosophy everybody can contribute for her own purpose. Today many people analyse the present time, and many problems need to be resolved according to this time; if the problem is in the present time, there is no need to bring in the old philosophy. It has been said that "the particular story of philosophy in America during the twentieth century to be told here, then, will be a story of the persistence of pragmatist themes throughout much of the century, while emphasizing the mid-century transformations that resulted from developments primarily in analytic philosophy. These combined influences resulted at the turn of the millennium in the flourishing, among other developments, of distinctively analytic styles of pragmatism and naturalism" (O'Shea, 205). O'Shea's essay determined that America came to impact the modern philosophy. The modern time was eager for certain developments in metaphysic because human beings are already developed, and this development requires something that can give solutions to the populations. The American continent is developing daily with new people that can contribute and update old philosophies. The past has already given the solution to today's period; the most important thing is to keep up with the new maxim, for the solutions of tomorrow. Many American philosophers worked very hard to bring up new philosophical ideologies in this modern time to benefit their people. There was still a problem in the past, but the philosophers in that period resolved the solution. Even now, America still has a major problem, and the philosophical problem cannot be resolved for only a particular group of people.

From time to time when there were the problems in America, they had to come together to create a platform that could help them to find the solution. It is always better for people to be represented together, for the purpose of the population. America came to challenge many philosophies in the early nineteenth century; this movement came from the many states in America. One of the reasons for that movement was for the development of philosophy and to give the opportunity to other philosophies to carry on the research. O'Shea argues that "this platform contended that the perpetual disagreements characteristic of philosophy, while due in part to its subject matter, are due "chiefly to the lack of precision and uniformity in the use of words and to the lack of deliberate cooperation in research. In having these failings philosophy still differs widely from such sciences as physics and chemistry" (O'Shea, 217). This unity brought the integrity and value of the population to the solution that came from the major philosophical organisations in America. The problems of the world cannot only come from a small part of life, but it can come from many parts of human beings, and human beings are responsible for their own solutions. If a human being thinks of determinism, there is no allowance for another person to come from afar and give the solution, because the owner of the problem believes he can understand his own problem better than others. The world has its own reality that requires human beings to think through to their personal lives rather than waiting for somebody else to give them the solution. As I said before, nobody else can understand my problem better than myself, because I am the owner of my personal life, and I know my own conscience. The medicine doctor cannot discover a symptom if I do not know say what I feel.

The European philosophy came from the Greeks; the majority of the European countries came together to develop that philosophy, and the solution was given for them to use Greek philosophy for their purposes. Europe consists of multiple cultures, and each country has its own major philosophical tradition. Europe accepts the external religions; this ideology came from the postcolonial period because many Diasporas have their own beliefs and traditions. The European philosophy brought the series of ideologies into the world, and those ideologies contributed to the world to categorise and to group the human races. The Europeans use scientific experiment to develop technology in the world. The ideology of democracy was made for equal opportunity; every human being in Europe has the dignity to live with the freedom of speech and liberty. The Europeans accept the ideology of naturalism because every European is capable of doing what he wants in order to survive. The European philosophy grows daily, and one of the reasons is because of the countries Europe colonised in the past. It has been said that "for most of us today, time is understood in terms of what it is to be on, behind, or ahead of time, where punctuality serves not only as the basis for time's measurement but also reflects an elaborate form of socialization: to be on time, be it for people or events, is distinctly modern urgency elevated to the rank of a social virtue" (Warren, 2009: 100). The concept of the European philosophy is to analyse the solution because every time there is a solution, the problem can arise at any time. Especially when there is a problem with immigrants, the European constitution must resolve that problem as soon as possible. Where there are human beings, there is always a problem because two people cannot have the same vision— their understandings are always different.

The philosophy of Europeans mixes with other people's philosophies because of the immigrants that come to Europe, and those people have philosophical aspects to contribute. In 2010, when I was in theology class, one of my colleagues came from England. I asked him where the Scottish came from, because he had the Jewish Scottish map. He was very angry and answered that there were many blacks in Europe, and I was lost completely at his answer. The Europeans are probably getting tired of seeing their countries invaded with many sorts of races. Many of the Diasporas are telling them that it is Europe that controls their own countries; particularly, African countries are controlled by European politicians. The problem is that most of them forget that as long as the world still exists, the number of people will increase because human beings were created for productivity. In science when something is productive, it cannot be limited; it needs to be taken care of. Even today, Europeans can be found everywhere in the world, even speaking other languages better than the people in that country, especially in Africa. Time does not wait for anybody, and the problem will be always raised in society. Warren argued that "phenomenology is a method of rendering the familiar strange in transforming what is taken for granted into a theme of reflection. As a first step towards the recovery of what we take for granted of time, Husserl argues that a phenomenological analysis must abstain from any reference to the 'existences' 'reality' of time. This demand for the suspension of time should not be conflated with a denial of time's existence" (Warren, 2009: 101). The existence of human beings is joined with time, and there are always three steps: born as a little baby, life experience, and consequences. This means that the body must be destroyed. All those steps function with time, unless one dies before one lives.

SECTION 4

The Cause of World Conflicts

a) The Wars

A war is always a method of creating conflicts in society. Many wars cause disasters among people, especially when another country does not have enough forces to fight back—and after the war, that country will not have the opportunity to progress. In today's world many countries still have conflicts that were caused by previous wars, and the civilians cannot cope to support the present time. The human mind can be destroyed psychologically because of war; this is why the damages from a war are always dangerous to people.

One day I was talking to one of my friends, and he said to me that I had to shout very loudly because he could not hear what I was telling him. In the war that took place in his country, somebody shot a gun next to his ear, and now he could not hear well. I believe that even his children had problems speaking to him, when he would start telling them about what happened to him and thinking about the incidents that had happened. Wars used to drive many people into difficult times, and when they start telling their lives during the war, it is always hard to hear about it because the wars left them with dangerous pain which they cannot forget. In the world there is nothing as bad as war. Innocent people die without cause; they always lose their purpose and right to live. When it comes to the biggest countries fighting each other, the populations do not have access to help anywhere in the world because of political issues. I know it is not good to say this now, but I have to say it: why don't the presidents, kings, and queens who cause the wars fight each other instead of letting innocent people die? One of the reasons is that they always scar the civilians—what is the point in letting people vote after you cause a war against those same people? This is another issue the leaders of all the countries need to solve, rather than letting the population die for rulers' personal interests.

The war business destroys many families. A lot of people do not want to die, but neither do they want to lose their projects and businesses because of war. When people lose what they have worked for, it causes bad feelings, and they cannot cope well in the future. Many wars have happened in the world, and those who have lost their possessions, houses, and businesses often do not get them back. It is always hard for them to get back what they lost, and sometimes even their own governments ignores them—in the countries where democracy or freedom of speech is not authorised, it is impossible. Wars cause a lot of damage, and this is very painful because the poor populations always lose, but the rich and the organisations that cause wars have the opportunity to benefit. Every time there is a war in a country that produces oil, gas, or anything that can contribute, the war's organiser benefits because in those countries the populations are distracted. Children lose their parents, and parents lose their children. It is a very hard time when there is war in a country. Everybody has the right to live; I do not think the poor people should be involved in war's business. Many people die because of politics. The bombs' chemicals can still affect people years later. The entire population is the war's victims, and many people become disabled. Families are split and cannot resolve their own situations. Even the governments cannot help them, and if those people will not get any help after the war, then what is the point to causing war in the first place? The entire world should analyse ways to stop the wars in the world; even rebel wars must be stopped. I believe that everywhere human beings live, there will be always the problems, but one should not kill the poor or rich because the problems will increase war.

Many people are the victims of wars. From time to time, the population increases, and the number of depression cases increase because of the wars' victims. Many people who are war victims suffer from depression. The sufferings from the consciousness used to come by telling the incidents of the wars, and the media and personal letters. When somebody is born from that family, that child will grow with the inner consciousness affected, and many young people now do not realise how their lives can be improved. One of the reasons is because if a parent is a war victim, a child is able to feel that suffering when the child is in her mother's womb. Many people are born with inner sufferings because of wars in their countries before they were born, and they have no choice but to change their nature because they did not choose to be born in that country. Wars are supposed to bring stability to the lives of humans, but the war today actually causes problems for many people. Even today, every time there is a war, there will be always the deaths of the innocent people who never knew the cause of the war. The innocent people become war victims from one generation to the next because history will repeat itself. Even the government of that country never has the ability to help the victims' families; this is ignorance from the government and politicians. They are always the first to promote damaging many families by declaring war, but they do not have the ability to restore families.

Atomic bombs cause many disasters in the world; to this day Japanese families still suffer from that incident. There was a story of a Japanese woman who was a war victim, and the war caused many incidents in the past in Japan. The atomic bombs were dropped two times, and many people's mental and physical states have been unwell since they were born. For the compassion of the war, they helped the woman's father with free medical treatment in Japan. Many people in Japan are second and third generation after the bombings. The suffering from their ancestors caused them to be war victims, but they themselves have never been where the bomb dropped. The atomic bomb damaged the bodies of many Japanese. When people realised the cause of the bomb, everybody started to panic. Many people lost their goods, and they did not have money to help each other; neither could their government help them during that period. Many people did not die in good condition—they were not buried in a good way, with the respect due to human beings. All these conscious pains made the Japanese victims of that war start telling their stories to their next generations. Many people in Japan where the bombs were dropped left with the scars in their bodies. They would also not forget about the incident, every time they saw those scars. Those scars would motive them to tell their children, who had never participated in the incident. Even the children who were born after that war still know about the incident, and it is a psychological problem. If the government of Japan does not do anything about those victims, there will be always the problems. When people listen to atomic bomb stories, they always find it is very important to hear them, and even watch stories in the media.

The pains and problems are still moving from one generation to another without any good solution. The number of the population is decreasing because of the wars caused by governments and politicians in the country. Many children from the next generation, who never participated in the actual conflicts, will not live a life of depression. Perhaps in a different country the children would live a life of vengeance. If the government is not capable of finding the solution for the next generation, everybody still has these incidents in their minds. If it was not an atomic bomb that took place in those villages in Japan, there would not be any problems because those war victims would have a better future. Imagine somebody who could deliver this world from the crisis also died in that village, or somebody very important in the world would have come from those villages—but that person is now dead. People might say that another person will be born in a different country; there is always a special person in a good place. The war is not the solution of humans, but according to this story, the war means the destruction of the entire human being, both spiritually and physically. It is always the spirit that controls the body, but the body does not control the spirit. When the spirit is destroyed, the entire body will also be destroyed. The war manifests in many ways. Many people today do not want to die in the wars, and one of the reasons is it is the organisation that controls the world and prefers to capture and condemn the leaders, rather than killing the poor people. Some of the population prefers that leaders die.

There was another war in part of Asia. This was a war caused by many incidents, and always people died without any good reason. The United States and the Soviet Union are the countries that cause the biggest wars in this world. They do not even think of the consequences; people die in many countries from a lack of law, but they deserve to live. Human beings are not materials—when the physical body is destroyed, there will not be anybody who can replace a person with the same spirit and consciousness. Those countries are the first to cause world wars in other nations. The United States and other countries should analyse their decisions before people die. They should also ask the opinions of each individual rather than asking representatives of the populations. I do not think that if somebody struggled very hard and bought a big house, then she would authorise people to break the house. I do not think anybody should tolerate this happening. America came to use the consequence of the wars' problems by killing leaders rather than destroying the entire population while looking the solution. Since Saddam Hussein was killed, the Iraqi population has never had peace because many people lost their lives, their families members, and their business. In Vietnam the population should have freedom of speech and the right to defend themselves; they had the chance to choose the right things or the bad things, and everybody has the right to choose something better. We should not impose wars on others. If they want to live in that way, who are you to go change them? What if their ancestors lived in that way for many years, and nothing bad happened to them?

The United States and the Soviet Union came to Vietnam with strong justifications: to convince the local population about their political business. The Vietnamese had a good amount of time before these wars started; they were doing their best to survive with their French connection, and the population did not do anything wrong. When America introduced their issues of politics, the population started to die in the war that was caused by America. The history about the cause of those wars contains many different interpretations, but the population did not have a choice whether to reject or accept the wars. I think that if they asked for each person to choose the war or reject it, the majority of the population would reject it, and they would request for peace. Christ Trueman stated that "the causes of the Vietnam War and the subsequent war itself were classic symptoms, components and consequences of the Cold War. The causes of the Vietnam War revolve around the simple belief held by America that communism was threatening to expand all over south-east Asia" (2000-2013). The problem will still arise as long as human beings do not have the right to live democratically. If everybody had self-expression in this world, many problems would have their solutions. The problem of the Vietnamese was not based on the financial crisis; it was political issues. However, all those incidents developed from war's symptoms. The Vietnam War caused also many families members to be separated. Many war victims, and sometime the organisations involved in that war, do not even talk or care about those war victims. If the Vietnamese people are suffering from many issues today, I think the cause of it was coming from the terrible war that happened in the past. The problem needs to be treated in order to find a good solution; those villages still have the story of that war, and sometimes they do not know what to do about war victims because they have been rejected by human rights organisations.

The solution to our problem is always among us. The problem is also among us, and they both are opposite from each other. Humans have their own understanding of living because of wars. But there is no need to change people regarding their ways of living; they are already used to their lives and cannot change. There are many wars victims in the world; each of the massive wars has made more than half of the population involved victims. Since the creation of human beings, they consciously cannot tolerate to die for something that they have done. In Vietnam there was terrible war that caused many victims; to this day there still are many people that suffer from those incidents, which damage many families in the Vietnam countryside. There are also many US soldiers who have problems from that war because there were many traps in the forests of Vietnam that killed US soldiers. I watched many documentaries about the Vietnam War, including the fictional movies about that war, and I always realised that there will be always the problems in the future. That war never ended like a normal war does, because of the separation North and South Vietnam. Also, the first country that occupied the Vietnamese was a different country, but the country that came to divide was an even different country; they signed the paper, but the war victims had something to say about the war. The problem keeps increasing rather than decreasing; the war in Vietnam could not bring the peace because there were deaths in many camps, including the US troops. Many soldiers after that war were traumatised, and their loved ones feel sad about what happened to them and their families. Many soldiers were also victims; even high-profile people in the United States were protesting, asking the government to stop fighting.

Many people become aware of the consequences of war because of the wars on the Asian continent and the victims of those wars. Every time when the government and the politicians want to cause the war, they always think of the disaster in the first place. I remember one leader in Africa who did not like to get power by shedding the population's blood, but when he was afraid to shed people's blood, then another person would come to take power by doing so. That leader was not wrong with his idea because he found the solution to keep the lives of the population safe. The Vietnam War caused damaged within the population, and many Vietnamese could not recover from their financial problems. There was an answer to their financial crisis. Everybody knows Vietnam is a country that develops agriculture, and those people in their villages could not find anything to eat. People had to abandon their homes because there was shooting all over the place. Nobody was born to live or die in wars. The psychological problems took place in Vietnam because many victims lost their goods, and families were separated because they were afraid to die.

At that time the French occupied the Vietnam, Vietnamese were also speaking the French language, but their neighbouring countries could not speak French, so there was a problem. The neighbouring countries had problems and were not involve in the war. The biggest problem was communication in that period.

Many terrify stories happened in the nineteenth century in Vietnam, as well as in other parts of the world. The incidents caused much death in the country of Vietnam, but people that caused those wars were not affected, and they sacrificed innocent people's lives. The wars which happen today are not made by the simple population. Imagine a poor family that lives in the countryside without any money to survive—we should ourselves how that family should cause a massive war. They do not have anything to do with the government and politics, but they are the first victims. The government and its institutions make the uncomfortable decision to sacrifice the lives of the citizens, and yet the families of the government workers and politicians do not fight because they are well protected. Many people can find places to hide themselves from the bombs, grenades, and bullets. If they have somewhere to hide, as the families of the governments and politicians, perhaps they will be very happy with the war.

Rape always takes place in many wars. It is one of the instruments that many people do not pay intention to or mention in war. When I was young, one of the soldiers from my country told me many stories about the war. That person said every time there was a battle, afterwards there was also raping of the females in the villages. I believe that, because a human being is an agent, and what another person is thinking, there will be also another person that is in a different place but would also do the same thing. There are also the women who are in labour during the war, but many people do not want to consider that. Sometimes the soldiers become doctors because some of them help the women in labour. Of course there is always the Red Cross organisation to have that responsibility, but in some countries the Red Cross is very poor due to a lack of the government's funding.

The war in Vietnam was not just to cause the conflict between North and South Vietnam, but to remove the French regime. The Vietnamese did not have these sorts of separation; they used to live that way before the war took place. The new world constitution made a conflict to challenge Vietnam's constitution and turn that into a conflict. The next generation will always have conflict with North and South Vietnam every time. According to several stories from Vietnam War victims, many people had nothing to do with the organisations that caused the war; they had also a choice to make the government respect human rights and to ask everybody his or her opinion. It seemed that even the Vietnam government was forced philosophically to accept the conflict between North and South in their own country. The human consciousness could not accept that the choice was made by superior organisations; the conflict of the North and South was not the solution, but it caused psychological conflicts in the families of many victims. Those who lost their family members still have the bad memories. Human beings cannot forget what they see. The conflict in war is always preserved in the future memorial. The problem is always found in the middle of the individual lives of each family in the country.

The war also causes culture conflicts. When the South fought against the North, this was also an ethnic war; the North part of the Vietnam also has an ethnic group. The soldiers and the politicians who were fighting each other belong to those ethnic groups. The solution could come when the war organisers have the ideology to not just stop the war but also consider that every human being has the right to give his opinion. It is not the organisation that represents human beings, but human beings themselves.

b) Interfering in Spiritual Matters

The act of interfering in spiritual matters is one method that many people use to learn others' religions, participating in their beliefs but not being a member of that religious group; it is different than observation. The world today is functioning in two ways, materialism and spiritualism, but the majority of people believe in spirituality only after they can analyse the material. Everything that human beings do always starts from the spirit before becoming real. Many singers and artists used to dream before they started telling others about their dream. In this section I will introduce the worldwide spiritual problem and the conflicts that used to occur. I believe if the world does not resolve the spiritual problem first, it will be very difficult to resolve the material problems. Many governments and politics ignore spiritual matters and only think of the material conflict.

The evolution of humans is to be born; after the body will be buried, where will the spirit go? There are many interpretations from many different religious groups. Some believe in rebirth, but how can they prove it? There are many questions that people ask, such as why anybody would chose to be reborn into a poor family. I think there will be many responses, and each person will experience them when he or she dies.

To interfere in another religion does not mean becoming a member of that religious group. Everybody in this world is eager to know other people's beliefs, and families can have the same religious group or diverse religions within the family. With diverse family beliefs, the majority often treat the minority faith poorly.

There are many religious groups that understand the spiritual matter differently because they believe that everybody has a right, and they allow everyone to contribute to society. Many people in the world today become more spiritual rather than being materialism. Sometimes the world believes that when the spiritual things are not working well, the physical will also manifest differently. Theos's report 2012 drew on data from an England-wide survey. "Theos published a short research report entitled 'The Faith of the Faithless'. This was found, among other things, that over a third of people who never attend a religious service express a belief in God or a Higher Power, nearly a quarter of atheists believe in a human soul, and around a fifth of non-religious people believe in the supernatural powers of deceased ancestors" (17/10/2013). There are also some people who normally work things out and find the solution without the help of any religious group, because they believe in themselves. Those people, with their confidence, have a reason to accept and support their ways and beliefs. Faith's motivation made them understand the problems that confront them. The world has no obligation to accept the solution that can come out of the spiritual religious group, and one of the reasons is that the solution and advice are based on spiritual matters. Conflict will arise every time when there are diverse problems, especially in a community where there is no luck for those who do not belong to any religious group, because these people won't be able to contribute their points of view. When human beings think of spiritual matters, there is always a possibility for religion to be involved, and the metaphysics of religion is that every human being is in search of something that he cannot see, but he feels there is another power that is over him. Many people feel rejected in their communities because of their personal beliefs; with spiritual interfering, those people need to be assisted because their ideas are very important and challenge those who are more spiritually aligned.

One of the spiritual conflicts is rebirth and resurrection, and most of the religions will never come together with one solution to the community. I believe that if today the world is not functioning well, it is because there are many issues which many organisations need to look at in every aspect of human life. Many people think that rebirth is not good because the spirit must leave a body to return to its creator. Another part of the faith believes that when somebody dies, that person must return again; this is a resurrection but is different from the Christian perceptive. Davies states that "in revolution times, as in all others, people die and have to be buried or otherwise disposed of. The benedictions and the blessings of ordinary funerals and services are echoed in prayers and in Jewish epitaphs discussed by Van der Horst: Here under the shelter of this stone, stranger, lies . . . Demas, deserting the old age of his very pitiable mother and his pitiable little children and his mourning wife" (1999: 110). The result after death is always personal. When somebody has not died yet, that person does not have any death experience, unless she dies and can come back to tell people. Even if such a person knows that she died and retuned back to life; the majority of people will not accept a person that allegedly returns back to life because they never had that experience themselves. The world's principles always look at the majority or quantity, rather than quality. The ideology of rebirth or resurrection always makes conflict in society, and this conflict comes from different spiritual analyses—and no spiritual analysis, such as atheists. It is very hard for people to spiritually understand each other because of their religious backgrounds, and everybody can express it differently. In rebirth or resurrection, the conflict does not stop because of the spirituality matter; everybody will come with her own understanding to interfere with the ideologies of reborn. Every community has its own faith belief, and when somebody is new, she comes to introduce new ideas in the community, but that person often follows the principles of that community instead.

The United Kingdom is one of the largest countries in Europe that has multiple cultures. There must be evidence of the conflict that is happening, and the problem can't be checked because many people cannot support it. The world is not working as before; people start dying at a young age because there is a problem in the family, and there cannot be peace. Marriages have becoming less valued, and divorce is taking place instead of working on the marriage. The problems without solutions separate the unity of the people. Many spiritual matters interfere in marriage problems; many people cannot have weddings due to the financial problem. Death becomes more popular than birth, and people do not want to give birth because of the financial crisis. This is a spiritual conflict. Many Churches in the UK believe that the number of funerals have increased more than marriages, and the churches' members also increased in number. Many people become jobless, and they start going to churches rather than staying at home and watching their televisions. The figures of divorces increased from 1980 to 2007. Many families started losing their family members at early ages; when somebody dies in the family, there is always spiritual pain, and it makes people feel bad. I knew a family that lost their father; they had to hide the children from that news because it might affect the children. After four years they created the maxim to inform the children about their father. The children were very happy, but it was too late for them to be affected with the bad news because they'd become adults. The spiritual interfering will cause many people to have conflict within their families, and many people are able to control them spiritually. Many people are lost because their leaders in the churches did not show them the right path to follow. Coaches, mentors, counsellors, and advisers are people that give people the right advice and also help in spiritual direction.

The world is becoming more frightened; there are many problems that develop every second and in every country in the world. The world conflict starts interfering within continents and countries; many families become unable to resolve the problems they are facing. There is no need to escape the world's problem, because humans were created to be productive in the world, but many countries think about how to stop that productivity. Abortion becomes the norm, but the problem is that people who authorise the killing of the foetus forget that they themselves were a foetus. I don't think any government has the power to authorise the killing of a foetus. Human productivity is unstoppable since the creation of the human being. These kinds of illusions are penalising many families in productivity; even the religious groups cannot say a word or oppose the law. Countries that make abortion legal do not require certain families to abort. If the couple wants to keep their baby, they do not have to have an abortion. The countries should give the population the right to keep the foetus rather than impose people to do the abortion.

Many laws come from the religious spiritual movement rather than the government or politics. The law will apply to everybody, including other faith beliefs, and it is always compulsory for everybody to obey. Today in the world, there are laws that can come from only one religious group, and it will cause many conflicts with other religious groups because all the religions do not have the same principles. The world cannot be controlled by only one law, because many people have their own ways of thinking and living. When a government starts to make conflict in religious groups, it's a spiritual matter, and there will be many disasters in the world. James argued that "I will add one more example, taken from modern French history, in illustration of the estimate of an oath held by Catholic priests. In August, of year 1790, 'the Civil Constitution of the Clergy' became law in France. The avowed tenor of this enactment-as its title indicated, and as its supporters formally announced-was in no way to invaded the spiritual domain f Church, but only to provide for the better civil organization of the clergy" (James, 2009: 156). Some of the laws are not too bad, because other people who belong to that particular law feel confident with that law. There is also the question as to whether that law is valuable to other religious groups. When a particular law comes from a particular religious group, it likely means that religious group is the majority in that country. There is no need to choose the government law from a minority religious group, because the entire population will be affected and more conflict will arise. Also, many people live spiritually in the world, and they express their lives spiritually in the countries from where they were born; their ways and belief are totally different from others. Ngunjiri argues that "Africa peoples all over the globe share a spirituality (not a religion) that has been recognized as distinctively Africa in its explanations of phenomena and its understanding of God as the definitive source and sustained of life" (Ngunjiri, 2010: 28). They believe that spirituality is very different than a religious group. Some people believe that religion can also be a part of politics. I had two hours to debate with one African who said that he was one of the Africa faith beliefs; it is not a religious group or sect, and neither was he an atheist. He said to me that Africa faith belief is a way of life.

Religious conflicts can occur in many areas of a spiritual life. The spiritual knowledge is one of the main parts of humans, but when there is a spiritual conflict, there must be also physical conflict because they two are parallel to each other. Most of the religious wars are spiritually based on the canons, and a contradiction of the belief can always occur. Those principles are always made and confirmed by a responsible community, and most of them used to have the inspiration from their own visions—and some from a philosophical ideology. In India there are the overseers that give a solution to the India population, and it is always mixed with a spiritual solution because Hinduism is more popular than other religions. There are certain rules that can be different than other religious groups, and some of the other religions find that rule impossible for them to practice because it conflicts with their spiritual beliefs. Because of that, violence occurs. Frykenberg argues that "it is possible that, as a result of the conflicts between heterodox Buddhist and Jain views and more orthodox Brahmanical institution, doctrines of non-violence (ahimsa) and transmigration (samara) found a permanent place within Brahmanical belief structures thereafter" (Frykenberg, 2008: 64). In the rules of morality, some people might be interested to see the inside of a certain rule for their population to practice. I saw a phone in China, and one could switch to somebody else's line off while he was using it. In the UK that sort of thing is not allowed.

The spiritual doctrines can be one the major conflicts in human society. When the majority of the population does not agree with a doctrine, it always causes division. Certain doctrines are also included within government principles, and most of the government agrees with the majority religious group. The religion that is most popular is always the religion that can have access to lead the country. The other religious groups that are not popular always oppose certain principles. When a government introduces a new principle, I believe that a good government prepares and analyses the rule before announcing it and enforcing that rule. To prepare the new rule or law for the country to follow, the government must consider all the institutions of that country, including religious institution for spiritual acceptance. If that country does not respect other religious groups, there is no need to consider the minority religious contribution. The spiritual conflict will occur because of the ignorance of the government: they do not consider the viewpoint of the other religions, and more problems will develop in that country. Some of the population will not be able to concentrate spiritually; perhaps they might not feel confident in controlling themselves spiritually. In every country there is always a religious group that is the most dominant; the less popular religions will always have difficulty in expressing themselves publicly. Even the government will authorise them to express their viewpoints publicly, but sometimes when these groups express their opinions, there will be a penalty and perhaps punishment and imprisonment. A spiritual conflict is very dangerous for the population because everybody belongs to or trusts in a particular spiritual belief or knowledge. It is always important for the government to try to analyse equal spiritual opportunity.

Spiritual conflict is the most dangerous part of human life. When the spirit controls the body, that spirit must be well organised without any disturbance. Many people in the world live spiritually, expressing their spiritual lives rather than their physical aspects, and there is no desire to stop mankind by being spiritual. When a continent or country is equal spiritually, it will develop, especially when there is consideration for other spiritual groups. Even the small spiritual groups have the opportunity to their feelings, and they have the right for their voices to be heard because they are also part of the country. Everybody needs a solution to the problem; there is nobody on earth who does not want a solution. Every religion in the country is very important because people who belong to that religion are also the part of the population. When the government decides to consider only the majority religious principles and apply them to everybody, there will be conflict and the population will be separated. Many people are dying spiritually and not just physically. Spiritually there is also a consciousness, and when the consciousness is not stable, the whole body will be unwell. The numbers of deaths are increasing, the numbers of marriages are decreasing, and many good things and opportunities that can contribute for the development of the country or continents are not improving. Money will not solve spiritual matters—the spiritual matters can only be solved spiritually. Then the outcome will be excellent, and the country will benefit from that excellent result.

c) Culture Imposing

In the world there are many problems that are involved in the cultures of countries. Most cultures have been affected due to the imposition of other cultures' principles. Some of the principles are not valuable to for other cultures and should not be mixed with others. However, some of the cultures can contribute to other cultures without causing any problems. There are many people who give their examples from another culture as the solution to their own cultures.

Many people do not tolerate other people introducing different cultures; they find them confusing, and introducing a different culture to people can cause trouble. Imagine people who have been living in a certain way for the rest entire lives, and then suddenly somebody else comes in with a new culture to challenge them and to tell them what to do. I think the world should think of many areas of life in which to find the solution. Today people do not find the solution because the majorities of the cultures have imposed upon the new cultures. Some of the biggest organisations impose upon the less powerful organisations, and that will always cause problems. Also, it always takes time for somebody to change quickly; every human being is difficult to adapt to new method as he or she matures.

The ideology of imposing on people new rules that they never used before will always cause social wars. In the postcolonial period there were always challenges of the various cultures because people were discovering each other. If the ideology of imposing the cultures of people still happen now, it means that the colonisation method is still the same, and they should change the system. Everybody belongs to a particular culture or ethnic group to follow instructions that belong to that group. When somebody changes his culture, there will be problems where some in society never respect his new culture. The culture is also an important part of social life that can bring the solution to the world; everybody belongs to a particular culture, and the leaders have also their cultures. Many countries or continents have multiple cultures, and those cultures have principles within them. There is no need to separate people who are in the same culture because of the imposition of a new culture.

A culture can also help the communication of a particular group. The groups can interact with each other in order to keep themselves happy, and other people from different cultures might also be interested in them. Every time there are numbers for a majority of people, there will be always the facet that connects people together. Communication is always good for people to speak one language; foods can be a major sign that identifies people who are in the same culture. A culture is a special area where everybody can be identified; it's used to help people know their background. Dialect is one sign that can identify somebody who comes from a particular tribe or subgroup. The names of people can identify those who come from a particular culture or tribe: many people that belong in the same social group have the same names. In Africa the names of people can identify the same people that come from the same tribes or ethnicity. Names also can unify people because when somebody is in a different country, it might get help from people that came from the same culture.

Character is also one of the main identifiers because many people who come from the same culture have the same character, and that character is always different than others. The world has many cultures, and when one culture is stronger than others, the majority of people will approach the strongest culture; this is where culture imposing will arise. Some of the cultures do not want to be imposed upon, and conflict will arise when there is refusal. It is always hard for other people to believe in a new culture because they have been used to their own cultures, with all the good and bad aspects. Their ancestors lived in those ways, and even if there are the errors which have been found, those errors will not make them change.

Many cultures start abusing and treating other cultures badly when imposing their own principles. People start to stand against any sort of imposition that can come to destroy them, but some of them take it too because they express anger and sexually abuse other—they forget human rights. To defend the cultures' principles, it does not mean one should kill people who misuse the culture's principles; rather, one should teach those people in an appropriate manner. If today people start killing whose who misuse a culture, the world will not have any human beings left. Some people think being aggressive is a solution to protect the culture, but it is wrong to force anybody with an ideology; forced people will not help the community. History will help us to understand the good and bad things about defending culture. Is it defence or abuse? To defend the culture, there is no need to abuse another person because many people do not rule other cultures from a different country. For instance, in Turkey there is a notice on the tourist buses that says if you see two men holding their hands and walking, you do not talk because it is their culture. In the UK they will call them "the guys". In the case Turkey's government does something that is illegal in the world, the visitors will be aware of the culture's principle. Everybody has the right to respect another person's culture rather than abuse or impose upon it. Since the postcolonial era, missionaries brought their own cultures, and their cultures were affected by others when they left. People are in charge of their own cultures by protecting the principles in many ways; it is not right to kill or abuse somebody for the misuse of a particular culture. People's cultures are supposed to be respected because the cultures are identifiers of people who belong to that country. Even people in the Diasporas have the right to express their cultures—but also the citizens need to respect others' cultures.

I would like to introduce an his incident because it is not copyrighted. I have watched a YouTube video and tried to translate it into English. This YouTube video was published to discourage racism in Russia in an appropriate way, because everybody does not approve of racist business. Perhaps you have read this, and you at this point you have found this information very harmful. But it is not that as bad as you think, because I have debated this part before I mentioned it in this part of my book. Everybody will be very interested to read this part of the book. I ask myself how many people are staying in good places and leading happy lives, but on the other hand some people are hostages emotionally, spiritually, and physically. We sometimes send our children to study abroad, but we have to be sure about where they are going, and our hearts must be there. Everybody on this planet has the right to live a good life, even people born into oppression or slavery. Life is for everybody who lives on this planet. Living abroad reduces the sense of understanding human rights, sometimes doing something that you do not do in the original country. Some people lose their rights by living abroad, especially when they meet the wrong people. Living abroad makes people reduce their superiority, and their authority will also be reduced. Many people who like to be superior to others never want to live abroad. I remember meeting people that had the best qualifications from their country, but after moving to a different country their qualifications were reduced because the system the new country did not allow them to have the same qualifications. I quote a comment from journalist Garcia, and I also debated the same story publicly; my analysis is in the public domain.

Finally, his captors force him to declare the phrase "White Power" in Russian to the camera. According to Buzzfeed, Smith filed a complaint with local police but was subsequently expelled from the university he was attending.

These Neo-Nazi thugs attempt to justify their violent attacks by claiming their victims are paedophiles while offering little to no proof. In several cases, they have accused their gay 15 and 16-year-old victims of being paedophiles.

"This thing of paedophilia that comes from the thugs and that is the excuse they use to justify their actions. They're neo-Nazi skinheads, the paedophile thing is just a ruse. It's a thinly veiled smokescreen for homophobic attacks," said attorney Coenraad Kukkuk.

According to a news release from the Sova Center which tracks violence in Russia, in October 2013, over 20 people were injured in racist and neo-Nazi attacks, two of them fatally. They also report that since the beginning of the year, racist violence has killed 18 people in Russia and injured 141. In its travel advisory, the State Department says non-white Americans have been "victimized in violent attacks by 'skinheads' or other extremists". (Garcia, November 6, 2013)

In my analysis, I did not want to introduce too much what Garcia said because he had many different opinions. I mixed up this analysis with the public analyses to make sense. I had many responses from people when I published this video on my Facebook page. The majority of people to whom I presented it found it very sad. It is not bad to show to people because it was part of the public opinion and was a philosophy analysis. The first things is the cause of the problem, because some people are the troublemakers; everybody is thinking differently, and so they must promote something. The Russian citizens have the right to react because they belong to that country, and they can do whatever they want to do when they are in their own homes. Even a dog does not beg when it is away from the house, or when the master is not there with it. This is true with humans, too: when a person is out of her house, she will behave differently. The solution cannot be found if there is no problem. When people are acting as police without official authorisation, that is very unlawful. I have seen it many times: when the police are chasing somebody, citizens also start chasing that criminal without the police's permission. One of the reasons the police does not want help is because one cannot trust a stranger person. <any people trust strangers and ended up regretting it.

Those people that kidnapped a black boy could not be trusted by the police, because in each country the constitution deals with different cases. This boy was abused by Russians, and they claimed it was because the boy was a homosexual. That boy was a black South African, and he looked to be twenty years old. I have watched this video and was traumatised to see how they were treating this poor boy. This boy was also a student at a university in Russia. The information about his friend and relative who lived in Russia was not revealed. He was tortured, his kidnappers called him a negro with no power, and they made him praise white people. Apartheid left South Africa

48

with a bad experience, and every time people remember the period of apartheid, it makes them unhappy. Now the boy's kidnappers were telling him to praise white power.

I put this on my Facebook, and one white lady looked at it and commented that she could not keep watching it. The future of this boy will not be good. He will tell his family, his children, and all his relatives about what happened to him that day, and those who listen to his version of the incident will tell others, and then the entire generation will be affected.

Populations live differently in their local communities. It is not the rules from governments that can bring peace or solutions, because many people still have their own strategies to destabilise government rules. That South African boy was treated badly, and he was not able to express himself freely. Many people understood this video and its many opinions; I was one of those who understood. The men did something bad that even their own cultures do not tolerate. I believe that there are even more homosexuals in Russia. Homosexuals can be found in many countries, but the citizens of those countries will not do anything bad to them. There has been a terrified reaction to the Russia kidnappers; they abused somebody that came to study in their country. That boy was a student and had the right to live like anybody else in Russia. If that boy was a homosexual, where are the other homosexual people that made love with that boy? Perhaps, they were also in Russia but hid. How did the kidnappers know that the boy was a homosexual, for them to say he was destroying their culture? I suggest that the local community in Russia live in the way that everybody used to live, to protect their local culture. According to Avruch, "Generic culture is a species-specific attribute of Homo-sapiens, an adaptive feature of our kind on this planet for at least a million years or so. Local cultures are those complex systems of meanings created, shared, and transmitted (socially inherited) our attention to universal attributes of human behaviour-to 'human nature'. Local culture directs our attention to diversity, difference, and particularism" (1998: 10). Russians have the obligation to respect other people's cultures and backgrounds in order to avoid quarrels with many people, because people are looking for the solution to how the world can be improved. Politically, today many countries do not want to express their bad behaviours to people who arrive in their countries, because many countries are becoming multi-cultures, and everybody has a right to express themselves freely and publicly.

In the future, many young South Africans will be afraid to approach Russia by themselves and without any support. They will need a good observation before going to Russia on their own. On the other hand, many Russians who are aware of this video will be embarrassed to see how their culture does not respect others, and they may try to show kindness to people who are coming to study in Russia. The Russian government should not tolerate this type of action, and I think the government should find these people and expose them in a public court to protect the dignity of the country. It is also dangerous for the Russian people who live outside of the country: many people will be aware of this incident, and there will be mistrust when somebody has a Russian friend or family member. Sometimes people do something bad that they feel is fine or defends their rights, but they do not want to analyse what other people might think about their action. I think that causes a bad reputation for the country in the future. This incident was not even confidential because it was exposed—they knew what they were doing because they were looking at the camera the whole time to tell that boy what to say to the nations. They made him speak something that is illegal in public, they insulted him, and they expressed their racist attitudes.

Character is something the world can understand in order to get to the solution, because the solution will not come simply from financial crisis with this matter; it does not require one to fill up the bank with money. However, there is a need of money to organise peace conferences to resolve this type of problem.

The culture cannot be represented by a particular group of people unless they are told to take an action representing that particular culture. When somebody represents a culture, it is always self-motivation, but it is not to be considered in public. Many people in the country have a right to defend their cultures in many ways—but not by discrimination because others will not be able to understand that sort of reaction. These groups should make an effort to not abuse people and to react in ways that are comfortable to everyone, by respecting other cultures. Avruch argues that "the second, psychogenic, reason culture is never perfectly shared by individuals in a population (no matter how, sociologically, the population is defined) has to do with the ways in which culture is to be found 'in there', inside the individual. Here are, broadly speaking, in the realm of psychodynamics, at least with respect to the ways and circumstances under which an individual receives or leans cultural images or encodements" (Avruch, 1998: 18). Everybody should respect other cultures, especially in the country where somebody is visiting; that country's culture must be respected, and the visitors should be practice or observe the culture as much as possible.

Everybody does not have the same culture or social life; the descendents of each country are different, and the way one country lives is not the same as the entire world. The world has many cultures, and those cultures should respect the others, which will help many people develop. But when it comes to abusing other cultures and imposing views on others, it will cause disastrous problems. Humans used to learn from several cultures, and people can do their best to respect others. We are living in modern times, and human can become more mature. Some other cultures are very hard to follow or to apply because of the principles used. Many cultures have powerful constitutions in certain countries: most of the laws in some countries are mixed with their ancestors' principles.

There is another way the culture of a particular country can be affected: by imposing on them through the government without the population realising it. These types of imposition or abuse causes trouble in the culture. Some of the countries from beginning of that country practice different characters, which they never learned from their ancestors. When they become adults, they will never tolerate people with a different way of living. I believe that it takes time for people to change, but sometimes when there is a group, the majority does not want to change, and there will be trouble in society. For example, there is no easy way for everybody to accept one person, because there will be refusal somewhere. I tried this many times, and when I say or think of something, I always think that I am right with my idea. When I test my idea in front of people, I am challenged because every human being does not think in the same way.

The ideology of imposition is not respectful of human beings in their own territory; it creates violence in the territory that belongs to other people, and to take that territory, there must be a civil war. Many people's cultures have been affected because of the imposition of strange cultures, and the people are doing something which they have never done before. The problems that are causing the failure of the world are not in one particular area; the problems can have solutions in many ways, and getting the solution doesn't mean simply concentrating on one point only. Culture is very important in our lives because we belong to different cultures; they are our roots, and everybody has them. It is very dangerous to challenge the entire country at one time. Everybody has a right to live according to his culture; if he does something wrong, and he will be corrected according to his culture. There are many people studying their own cultures in order to keep them moving forward.

Today in Africa there is more conflict, and it is because of the imposition of certain rules that affect many rules from different countries. I have been asking many Africans who live in Europe or the United States whether they have gone to any of those parliaments to change the European or US constitution. Everyone responds no. Even those who work inside their constitutions have difficulty in making certain rule changes. Many people think that colonisation is over, and people are back to their own businesses, but this is a mistake. I was very surprised to see President Obama react that way by bringing a new culture into modern times, because people have already adapted to live in a certain way for years. It takes time for people to adapt a new ideology or system, because the information used to pass from one way to another way. It is not just about giving a speech publicly so that some people might be traumatised or hear something new. Perhaps in the future an Africa president or king will travel to the United States or Europe to introduce African culture by forcing them to dress or eat as an African. Even in the airport, they do not authorise African food to enter, and people must hide African food or bring it in different way. The people on this planet has their own choices. What about a huge country with a multitude of people in it? Each individual has his choice to make, and the majority will not obey one person's choice.

Nossiter stated that "it was hardly surprising that a day after President Obama, in front of hundreds of reporters, traded barbs with President Macky Sall of Senegal on the topic, people on the street, the press and the radio in Mr. Sall's country lined up firmly on the same side" (June 28, 2013). The President of the United of State came to impose upon the population of the Senegal, asking them to legalise homosexuality. That is something that never happened legally in Senegal, and there were not even interest in marriage between two men or two women. The danger is that Islam is the majority religion of the population. Perhaps change might come in the future, but Islam does not allow homosexual marriage, and it would take several years for this issue to be resolved. Christianity has always tolerated many things, and I believe that if the majority of the population of Senegal were Christians, they would be very happy to allow homosexuality to take place Senegal. Senegal culture is very different than the principles Obama was imposing them, and to impose on people something that they have never done before is always hard. People may not adapt to that principle, and most of the population could cause a civil war. Their ancestors never lived with homosexuality publicly; perhaps some of them were homosexual, but certainly not the majority. The generation on which Obama imposed do not have an idea about homosexuality, especially the children, because many Africa children do not do something unless they learn it from their parents. When I watched this video, I looked closely to see that even Obama did not have a way to convince them; the president of Senegal rejected it by saying there were a lot of things they need to look at regarding the policy of the culture.

Since the postcolonial period, they are imposing on many countries in order to get access to colonise them. It is always better to change people's language before changing them. The introduction of the new culture cannot be introduced in the manner that President Obama tried with Senegal. It seems the United States violated a Senegal policy, and Obama did not respect Senegal culture. To introduce people to a new culture is not necessary for a president of a different country; instead, it should be the organisation that is responsible for the culture.

Everybody has the right to express a culture that other people do not know, or to introduce a culture that can help others to develop. The bad thing is that when somebody wants to shut down the culture that people have already used, the people will not be able to progress because the culture educates people from their backgrounds. Especially in Africa, culture is the most active aspect because it is always updated in terms of its respect. Many people of Africa respect and follow their cultures even when they are abroad; they still keep their knowledge and do not want to copy other cultures. The respect of the African culture can be found in marriage traditions. Africans respect the conditions of the culture, and there have never been homosexual marriages in Africa. When President Obama went to Senegal to impose respect of homosexuality on them, he forgot to think that in African culture, there is no homosexual principle because most African countries live according to their ancestors' principles. Avruch argued that "to ignore local cultures is to rely on a theoretically overdeveloped and deterministic concept of human nature that erases the observable facts of cultural variability and in practice usually ends up meaning, as Clifford Geertz once put it, that everyone else is less well got-up editions of ourselves" (Avruch, 1998: 10). For people to accept the imposed culture, it requires personal acceptance because in this modern time, people rely on choice rather than general imposition. In my book *African Inter-Religious Dialogue: Philosophy and Theology,*

I talked about the philosophy behind Africa voodoo, because African culture is always based on spirituality, and most of the spiritual factors come from African ancestors. For them to change something, they always ask for the elders to say something about that subject. However, the president or other politicians have no right to decide for the public. Today many problems arise by introducing cultures that people do not want to practice.

Normally finding the solution of a culture does not involve imposing on people a different culture that they have never before used. The problem of the culture does not mean the politicians or the government should give the solution. In Africa, the culture relies on the chiefs of the villages to sort them out. I had a discussion about culture with many different people in Africa, because they think the problem of cultures is for the government or the politicians. After much discussion, I realised that the African problem needed to be resolved by the villages' chiefs because they are the ancestral keepers of power. Homosexuality is not Africa's culture because they never acknowledged it since the creation of the Africa continent. The majority of the Africa population is the Bantu, and they are the type of people who practise polygamy rather than homosexuality. The imposition is always very dangerous for people to accept; even when the missionaries were working in Africa, they found the Africans very hard to understand, not because of the language but because of the culture differences. The United States should understand that people have the right to do something rather than having something imposed on them that is very taboo in their cultures. African culture is always mixed up with Western culture; marriage in Africa is already affected, but Western life is not affected. The cultures are changing, but people do not want to change because of certain rules, and they will not have the ability to survive. Marriage is one of the examples that represents Africa's culture: today African marriage is about symbols, but now it is also about Western currency. Africans do not even know when their currency will have value in the European countries and in the United States. Also, the African qualifications to be valuable in the

United States and Europe without judgement should be taken into consideration; then many people in African will be very happy.

d) Religious Conflict

There are the main religious groups that are more popular in the world today, and many countries' constitutions rely upon them. Islam is one of the religions that cover many areas of the continents Africa and Asia; they can be also found in the United States and parts of Europe. The Muslims also contributed to other religions for peace or ideas to develop a particular country. The Islam population can be also affected by many areas of human society because every human being carries his attitude from where he was born, and he introduces that in the community where he is currently living. Islam understands that every human being has a responsibility to do what is good. According to Islam, it is better for the development of the world.

Every human being has a right to understand his personality, and the governments of each country should respect everybody as a human being, because people have the right to make their choices. Singer argues that "the human quality that encompasses the concept of the ideal ethical value in the Quran is summed up in the term taqwa, which in its various forms occurs over two hundred times in the text. It represents, on the one hand, the moral grounding that underlies human action, while on the other, it signifies the ethical conscience which makes human beings aware of their responsibilities to God and society" (Singer, 1993: 108). People can publicly express themselves regarding a situation in the country, and even in the world. The Islam philosophy contradicts other religions because some religious groups' philosophies are different. What if in the same country, they use some of the religious groups' principles that are different than Islam? I think that there will be conflict in that country. It will be better when the government observes and considers the other religious groups' principles, for the sake of peace.

There is still a major problem in Islam regarding women as a priority. In many circles of Islam, a woman is useless and should remain speechless according to tradition; even in the mosque, they do not authorise a woman to talk. In the mosques the women are allowed to sit at the back of every man, and they must cover their heads and faces. No other men can see their faces.

Lehmann and Mohammad argue that "Historically, the practice of polygamy existed before Islam without restrictions. Islam limited the number of wives to four and established clear rules and regulations for the practice to ensure fair treatment of each wife" (2011). Today in certain countries where there are more than one religious groups, if the governments accept only the criteria of Islam to be considered in the constitution, there would be a serious conflict with the other religious groups. Many people from other religious groups would not accept that easily. There are many religious groups that are suffering where Islam religion is the majority, because Islam will not yield any control. The Muslims will not authorise other religious groups to express their rights. Many people are suffering because of religious principles, and some people need their religions to have responsibilities in the country where they live.

Marriage will be changed according to modern times, because in the new generations people will come to understand the Islam tradition in many different ways. Human beings are still multiplying in many other places, and they have their own cultures. In culture there is always different understanding of the principles, and many of the religious groups' principles are mixed with various cultures. When a religion is mixed with a culture, the principles of that religion may be affected. Many of the Muslims have problems financially in terms of individual possibilities, because everybody in the world does have the same amount of money in the bank account. In Africa where it is a struggle to survive, there will not be any occasion to force somebody to get more than one wife when he does not have the ability to support them, because in Africa most of women depend heavily on men. South Arabia is the richest country in the world because the majority of the population has a lot of money; this is one of the reasons that Muslims have more than one wife in South Arabia. Muslims do not want their wives' faces to be exposed in public, and according to psychology, this behaviour indicated that the Muslim men are very jealous of their wives. It is a bad idea to be jealous of someone that like. Jealousy can also show if one really likes someone. It is Islam tradition that woman are always inferior to a man; in Judaism tradition, it means there is always somebody above every human being, and even the men must cover their heads. The religion or culture used to come after somebody's choice, because everybody has a choice. That choice is determinism, but it is still a choice. When somebody is making a choice, that person can communicate with others by looking at and others' traditions and principles. People always make a decision on their own with freedom; the choice is always inside of somebody's heart, and nobody else can see it if that person has not said it.

The psychotherapy of religion is when a group of people can legally make their personal understanding into a practice. Somebody might have something that he was born with it, and he can express that within the group of people. People have the right to come together to express their needs. When somebody is expressing his idea, the people will be able to help that person improve. When somebody does not have the liberty to express what he knows, people will not be able to understand that person because nobody can read what is inside somebody else's heart. Many countries in the world have main, popular religious groups on which everybody can rely and trust. I always appreciate the definition by James Williams, who stated, "I now ask arbitrarily to take it, shall mean for us the feelings, acts, and experiences of individual men in their solitude, so far as they apprehend themselves men in their solitude, so far as they apprehend themselves to stand in relation to whatever they may consider the divine. Since the relation may be either moral, physical, or ritual, it is evident that out of religion in the sense in which we take it, theologies, philosophies, and ecclesiastical organizations may secondarily grow" (1982: 31). If there is religious conflict today, it is because many issues are not being agreed upon by the religions, because the world functions spiritually and not physically. The conflict can arise when certain rules that have been accorded by the religious followers are not what everybody expected. Due too many religious groups in one country, there will always be conflict because the religious group's principles are different from others. Many people are born in the same religious group until they become older; they live according to their religious group's principles, and there is no need for them to be separated from their religion. The religious conflict caused many divisions in societies both locally and internationally. There is also a rebellious nature that causes other people to create their own religions because they have been abused by others.

The religious groups cause many conflicts, and these conflicts lead populations into wars. The importance of the religious group in the country is not just to allow the members to express their personal feelings, but it is also to communicate with the world because the world needs the religious group for contributions in society. World conflict always comes from religion because many people in the world become untrustworthy, and that is why a religion is the only place for people to understand things spiritually. The world has many religious groups, but there are only three religions that symbolise those religions. The Abrahamic religion is one of the main keys that can help the world to understand the principles and needs of all the religions in the world. Many people are becoming more religious through their family members, but they are not practicing religious—they just want to be publicly seen that they belong to certain religions. These kinds of people do not respect the religion's principles; they always bring deception to the world, and many religious groups are having the same problems with these "followers". The world is developing day after day and in many ways, but the religions are now struggling to find the way out by setting up new principles to win over different conflicts to help the public. Religious conflicts can occur when there is a mixed religion situation, especially if two persons come from different backgrounds and struggle to understand each other. Many mixed-religion marriages have a lot of conflict because the religious principles are always different. Many marriages don't last long because of religious conflict in the community; especially when a husband is in the religious group that his wife does not want to trust, there will be terrible conflict. Problems will arise in the community. Thought there will be always the mixed-religion marriages, many families separate because of this situation.

According to the couple from a religious background, there will always be a problem with the marriage, and many couples have their marriages break down because the couple belongs to different religious groups. I know many people from the Islam background get married to people with a Christian background. My stepdad was a Muslim, but we were a Christian family, and things changed in the house, such as the observation of Ramadan (thirty days of fasting). I personally did not have a choice to do Ramadan because I was very young person. I followed Islam, my mum was into Islam, and all my young brothers were into Islam. When I grew up, I decided to leave Islam because I had a right to choose a religious group that I wanted. My family and I decided to make our own decisions. My friend in Pakistan always tell me that his friends from Islam tell him that they get married to Christian ladies in Europe and the United States. I answered him that it is always Europe and the United States that let people to express themselves without any judgement; their laws permit everybody to choose his own religious group, but on the condition that everybody must respect the government's laws. These two continents are based on Christianity, and the Christian marriage is always based on the Bible's principles. The church leaders do not have to be married before to bless the married couple, and some of the churches require baptism before marriage if the person has never had one. Now, when a husband comes from Islam, then his wife's family's religion that is different than Christianity will have the baptism to fulfil the marriage requirement. A Christian woman can easily accept Muslim men for marriage, but it is very rare to see a Muslim woman accept Christian men for marriage. The Christian women are very emotional; most of the Christian churches have many more women than men. But it is very hard to see a lot of the Muslim women in the mosques, just the men; I know because every Friday I always see the men outside the mosques.

The goodness of religion is that everybody in the world must live in the life that he needs to live, and it is not necessary to stop somebody to express his feelings publicly. When the religious followers are connected to certain politics, it makes sense because everybody deserves to live happily. Most of the contributions that religious groups make to government laws are in the image of unity, love, and peace. The population must feel free to be members of certain religious groups; each person has the right to join a religious group. The world needs the contributions of religious groups to solve many problems. If today there are problems in the world that need solutions, it means that the religious group is also part of the world solution. Religion has a major role to contribute: almost 99 per cent of the population belongs to a main religion in the world today. The majority of the population joins a religion because it is a place of refuge and self-expression. Most people become more spiritual rather than scientific because they realise that scientists cannot find all the solutions. Most people need religion because religion is the main solution in the world today. When somebody is looking for the solution, she often consults a psychic or a spiritual leader in her religious group to help her. People join religions just in case there is a problem. Religious followers can be very aware of the reasons why people are attracted to the religion. It is the influenced organisation which the religion is expressing in the world, and the religion in the community helps in many areas of human life.

Persecution is always very bad in a community because it causes certain religious groups to work against each other's freedoms. The religious group that persecutes others is usually the majority religion in that country. I went in Israel and saw how Islam was more popular than other religious groups such as Orthodox; even Judaism is less popular than Islam. The Muslims in Israel block the twelve gates of old Jerusalem; they said it's because Jesus will return to those doors, according their histories. The Muslims buried their dead bodies in an easterly direction, in front of the twelve gates; they said that when Jesus returns, he must take them first to heaven. The Christians cannot stop them from blocking those twelve gates because there are not many Christians in Israel to stop it. If the Christians break those twelve gates, the Muslims must prevent them from destroying those walls. In Christianity there is still persecution from within: Orthodox Christians do not really approach certain rules in the same manner as other Christians. There was a marriage in the Baptist church that was localised in Canaan, where Jesus did his first miracle. A man said to me that they wanted to get married, and they asked the Orthodox priest to help them with the proper marriage certificate from the Israel council. But when they asked for the permission from the Orthodox church for the marriage ceremony blessing, the Orthodox church refused because the bride was wearing a marriage robe. This was persecution because they rejected them, and the couple still feels pain about the incident. Many problems in religions arise to destroy communities. Religion is a system that can give peace and unite people because there is a place for all people to express themselves. Today in the world, many people are experiencing conflict because of religious groups.

Jackson argues, "In order for a human relationship to be correctly classified as a 'marriage', certain components must be in place. First, the marriage, is a relationship between a man and a woman. Increasingly, a degenerate world is pushing for same-sex 'marriages'. Who knows what may become 'legal' before this mess is over; whatever happens, Sodomite unions will never be 'marriage' with the approbation of Heaven" (2013).

Christianity views the marriage differently than other religions, expect for Judaism. Most Christian marriages are based in the Church; the Christian always thinks marriage is a blessing from God, and nobody else except God that can bless somebody to get married. Christian tradition condemns premarital sex because Mary and Joseph never had sex before Jesus was born. This is totally different from Judaism's understanding of marriage, because Judaism never believed in Jesus. Most of the Christians today do not authorise polygamy; Christianity condemns that view of marriage and says that a man should have only one wife.

Christians often condemn homosexual marriage; there is always a big debate within many Christianity denominations about that sort of marriage. Some of them believe it's okay, but some of them do not want that sort of marriage to take because they strongly believe in the literal meanings from the Bible. Today many denominations had divided, and homosexual is one of the main reasons for that division. Some people even get married with animals; some of them are Christian. From the other religions such as Islam, there is no homosexual marriage. Perhaps in the future many institutions will need to be modified. Even in Christianity, there was the proposition about homosexual marriage, but today it is becoming legal. We cannot refuse, but we can suggest and give people the answer in appropriate ways, because everybody has a choice as to what he thinks is right. The Christian religion gives authority to the husband to be the chief of his wife, and one of the reasons is that God created Adam first and then created Eve. Islam also has the same understanding of that authority principle: a husband must have authority over his wife. I always think about the marriage between homosexuals—how do they arrange the authority? Who is to have authority over the other?

Christianity challenges many cultures and communities in this world. Many people joined Christianity with their entire families. The good thing about Christianity it that people have the liberty to join Christianity and leave whenever they want. There is no need to force people to leave or stay; after leaving Christianity, they will be charged, and there will be a punishment during Judgement Day. Most of the Christian families have a mixed religion because in Christianity, there is freedom of expression, unlike in Islam. When somebody leaves Islam, that person must be persecuted when he joins another religion, especially Christianity. There are many people who are victims because they left Islam.

Singer argues that "the Jewish faith is a strongly ethical one, quite unlike the various mystery religions which were current in the Roman Empire at the time of Jesus. So it is no surprise that the Christian faith is also strongly ethical. Its sources are found first of all in the Bible"

63

(1993: 91). Christianity has a right to develop because it is a child of Judaism; it means that the majority of the principles can also be found in Judaism as well as in Christianity, but in a slightly different system. In the Christian marriage, it was first in the form of polygamy because of Judaism's traditions, and most of the Christian scholars of the Old Testament did not have too much information for people to understand about the Christian marriage. Christianity is already one step ahead because many Christians prefer to have only one wife or husband, and they also go the Church on a regular basis. I think if Christianity sets up the marriage rules for the entire world, many religions will be affected, and it will result in the conflict. There will always be conflict about marriage when a couple comes from different religious background, and they should have a good strategy to solve their issues.

Some religions authorise other religious believers to marry somebody in their religion without any conditions. There is no restrictions on the belief because a human being has a choice and the liberty to choose what is right and wrong. In the future, for the religions that prevent somebody from the different backgrounds to get married, there will be some confusion. Many people start to develop because of the technology that we are using; even where technology is not becoming aware, human feelings and sense can confirm that the world is changing without somebody else stating it. Walshe states, "Setting aside all ideas derived from other sources, other religions and philosophies of life, what is the Buddhist attitude towards marriage? For many Buddhists, in the East or the West, there is no great problem. They live a reasonably normal married life just as do many Christians, humanists, and others. We may say they are lucky, or enjoy the results of favorable kamma in this respect. For others, of all creeds or none, serious problems arise and must be somehow faced" (2006). The solution to marriage should come from the couple because they know each other better than anybody else, but it is always unthinkable when the institution starts to impose certain rules on marriage.

We may not say that Buddhist marriages should be the same as Christian marriages, because their way of worship is different. Their belief is different, and most of them do not believe in the person of Jesus. Philosophically in both religions the form of marriage might be the same, and there is always a reason for marriages to meet the same criteria. Regarding the marriage, a human being never has a specific decision that can help him understand marriage, because everybody has his own choice to make. If the Buddhists accept easily Christian marriage, it means the Christian ideology is the same as Buddhism—but when it comes to divorce, and is a different matter.

Many Christians should have access to marriage with Buddhists; they should be fine when it comes to belief, and the principles will not be affected. The reason why they will not be affected is because according to Christianity's principles, when a couple agrees together, there will not be a spiritual division. They are together physically *and* spiritually—that is the Christianity marriage principle. As far as the marriage principle is concerned, they will become as one person spiritually, and it is the spirituality that reassembles them. The marriage is something that should not have certain principles restricting people from getting married—otherwise there will be a lot of single people, and parents would not exist. Marriage is the duty of love, and the relationship has an obligation to have commitment for life because humans are made to be productive. In that principle of productivity, something can control it and secure it, because everybody deserves to be loved and trusted. There are people who refuse to have marriages with people that they know. Also, there are many religions that are not listed here, and they always allow marriage with somebody from one's own religion.

The philosophy of the Buddhist marriage is almost the same as Christianity, but not with all the principles. Christianity does marriages on the basis of the church. The Buddhist religion is spread among many places in the world, and the members also prefer to understand the marriage in their own ways. Many Christian traditions do not permit more than two divorces; perhaps it might happen in different ways, because much of Christian tradition is mixed with various cultures' principles. The Buddhists have the right to accept divorce in the church or civil council; it depends on the circumstances of the couple's choices and decisions. Some religious groups come with decisions or principles that are similar to other religions. The world today has many problems, and those problems need to have solutions to help communities, and even the entire country might benefit from the solution that will come from religion. The problem that marriage can cause in Buddhism is based on where they community is located; as I said before, cultures also affect religious groups. There was a rich African person who was living in Belgium for years, but he decided to bring his mother to cook *fufu* for him. According to his African culture, that rich man preferred his mother cooking for him because many Africans have a deeper love for the mother than the wife.

Buddhism brings the liberty of expression to marriage because it has fewer conditions than other religions, and many people can feel comfortable in a traditional Buddhist marriage. Buddhist believers will not have any conflict if they follow the principles of other religious marriage conditions; sometimes people have conflict due to disrespecting their rules and applying those rules in their lives. If a Buddhist wants to perform better in the marriage, he should confront the Monck to get instruction, or he can also change his beliefs because everybody person has a right to live in the way he wants.

Buddhism came with a philosophy of self-expression because it is a religion that considers the consequences of situations such as marriage. Buddhism is based on the action of the marriage rather than the outcome. Everybody who belongs to Buddhism has the freedom to have a marriage with a Christian in the church without any problem. Singer argues that "philosophically, the first prerequisite for a system of ethics, according to the Buddha, is the notion of free will, secondly the distinction between good and bad, and thirdly the notion of causation in relation to moral action. The third concept, as indicating the good and bad consequences of actions which can be morally assessed. is also related to a specifically Buddhist notion. Survival after death"

(Singer, 1993: 61). A couple should look at what is right and wrong in order to perform their marriage and to live good lives. Everybody has the right to observe the marriage in an appropriate way, and in a Buddhist marriage there is no the limitation for somebody to make the decision to stop the marriage. In the Christian churches, most of denominations do not allow many divorces. One person said that in some of the Pentecostal churches, they do not allow single people to take responsibilities in the church. The philosophy of Pentecostalism is based on the Bible's principles rather than Buddhist ones, because they deal with the consequence of a situation. In Catholicism, most of the priests do not want marriage because of the Catholic principle; in Pentecostal, they will call the priests of the Catholic irresponsible if they are *not* wed. If in the future Catholics will authorise priests to have a legal marriage, and then I think Pentecostal and Catholic will have a good relationship. Buddhists can relate to Christian marriages; it is Islam that is very different in marriage because they allow polygamy.

Christianity is based on self-control. Everybody has a right to defend her personage and respect the commandments of God. Christianity marriage is always based on faith, requires Christian instruction, and is family process. A Christian person that has a large family will not tolerate her marriage to be celebrated without a family ceremony in the church. Those who do not have a large family but with have a large number of friends and relatives will also have a large ceremony. The Christian marriage and the Buddhist marriage have similar principles because Buddhism tolerates their believers to have marriages in the church, with Christianity's principles. When there is a mixed marriage between a Buddhist and a Christian, the Buddhist will rely on Christian principles without any problem. It has been said that "is the distinction between killing and letting die, or between active and passive euthanasia, morally significant? Is killing a person always morally worse than letting a person die?" (Singer, 1993: 297). One can suggest that the idea of divorcing by error cannot help the mixed marriage between Buddhist and Christian in terms of loving one another. Both religions believe in what they do because of the acceptance of their marriage principles. Many religions prefer not to marry somebody from another faith. But as far as Christians are concerned, everything must be done in love according to 1 Corinthians 16:14; refusing somebody in marriage because of her religion leads to the death of that person's heart. God is the author of the marriage, and according to the calculation, no human being will live for 201 years on this planet earth. As far as Christianity is concerned, there is no refusal of marriage to people from different backgrounds, and it is a religion that welcomes everybody with love. Even in the countries where Christianity is most popular, there will always be a respect of other religious beliefs rather.

SECTION 5

World Economic Crisis

The world economic crisis is normally a brief economy crisis. Many people today are affected due to the crisis, and there are many problems in these families that can occur. If today there are divorces because of the crisis, the question is always how the family can survive without financial problems. Many families have been dispersed and cannot come together anymore. In the countries where they rely on other countries' power, there is no psychological or philosophical problems; people are looking for the solution everywhere. As I said before, when there is a problem, there is also a solution because they walk together and are parallel. There is an image that can demonstrate to people that there is still a solution, even there is disappointment first. In a human being's mentality, when there is a problem, automatically somebody will think of a solution. The financial crisis is a serious disaster and has caused the deaths of several people; it also causes divorce. When people start destroying each other due to a lack of finance, how are those people going to find the solution? Perhaps the person that they destroyed would have given them the solution.

a) Continents

The African continent has many types of cultures, but despite that it is always depending on Europe and America for aid. The continent of Africa has a duty to think of its own future. Africans should know consciously that the postcolonial period has already done its job, and it is now time for them to develop. There is no need for Africa to be always affected by so many things. What if there was no Europe or America? How would the African continent survive? In the continent of Asia, when there is a problem, they always run to their elders to help them. The African continent is different: when there is a problem, they always complain that they are postcolonial problems, and Africa needs to search for its own colonisation to get help. It has been said that "while financial needs to mitigate the economic and social consequences of the crisis are substantial, they must be met. Africa cannot be left alone, or viewed as the last priority, when it comes to dealing with a crisis which originated elsewhere in the developed world" (4.3 Substantial financial needs African Report: Development Bank 2009). If Africa has a problem with the financial crisis, one of the major reasons is because Africa's financial situation is kept in the occidental banks rather than in Africa banks. People in Africa are suffering because the governments are not doing the right things; the African governments have a duty to be transplanted with the population. Africa's financial crisis is not stable because African governments are not making any effort to develop financially for the benefit of their people, and most of the leaders work for their own pockets. The African governments let their own populations suffer for the leaders' own glory; every African president uses the population in this way.

BBC News stated that "the former president of the Central African Republic, Jean-Bedel Bokassa, has been formally rehabilitated by presidential decree. President Francois Bozize published the decree as part of the country's 50th anniversary of independence, returning Bokassa 'all his rights'" (2010). President Bokassa was not even supposed to be called a president, but an emperor. It is not because he is already dead and there will not be such a president, but Africa still has many of them, with different methods of applying the title of emperor. After him there always be emperors, but they use a different title because the entire world does not agree with this type of behaviour. Imagine somebody that controls the entire country and has seventeen wives; every African woman, when she is married with a rich person, will be taking the money from him to give to her family. Most African men help their wives' families rather than their own proper families. In this case, with somebody like Bokassa, his wives need money to help their families, and his own money goes to helping the families of his wives. How can this kind of person help and think of the population when he is paying for all his wives? In order for him to help the population and come out of the financial crisis, he had to abandon sixteen of his wives and be left with only one. Most African presidents kill everybody that opposes them in the country; if they cannot kill them, then they must abuse them. Bokassa was feeding his animals human flesh. When a leader is killing his own population, how can that population love its leader? When the president kills people, what population will that president lead? He will not be able to lead anybody. There will always be conflict between the population and a leader. Africa still has many years to change consciously, and it might change many presidents, but if they still have the same mentality, then nothing cannot be improved. Africa gets help from the occidental nations as usual because the West is a place that Africa uses in order for the population to grow.

The Asian continent is the biggest continent in the world, with its subcontinent India. It is also the continent that has the largest number of people, and when there is a financial crisis, many people are affected there. The financial crisis is always a disaster for everybody in the world, but people also need to understand how the financial situations of their countries are functioning, because they are also allowed to know about the development of their own countries and compare it with others. The banks are the sources on which the population of a particular country rely, and everybody on the Asian continent has the privilege to save and manage their money in banks. By saving money, they can help many people acquire their interests, because everybody needs to get interest, especially people on pensions who always need help. Most of the poor in Asia used to live decently, when the finances in their countries were stable. Education always benefits from the good guidance of the financial district, because the student will be very happy to get good funds from their bank in order to pay for school. The bad news is that when there is a financial crisis, it is very difficult for the system to function, and a lot of people cannot cope as before. Many Asians survive in the business district; it is a continent that helps the rest of the world in business. When there was a financial crisis, the population of Asia was not happy. The banks in Asia could not function very well, and the banks' customers did not know what to do at that time. The customers could make noise to the banks because they were consciously aware of the incident, and money was taken out of the population. The Asian banks could not lend money for a period of time, and there were always the questions as to whom the bank was going to lend the money to first? There is no need for the populations to rely on their banks because of the incident; the population should able to struggle very hard for their financial situation.

Pomfret argued that "over the last decade Kazakhstan's economy has been the success story of Central Asia" (EUCAM Report, 2009: 3). From time to time, the financial situation was fine, and many people were living the good life. Many countries did not need financial support from other countries because they were depending on their own financial resources, and the population had no intention to go out of the country to settle. The banks were fine in the past before the financial crisis, and the population relied on their local and national banks because they had the privilege to borrow any amount that they needed. Everybody in the country had a right to live according to the principles of the government, which was leading the country. The banks were increasing every day because they had nothing to lose due to their clients depositing savings. When people save money in the banks regularly, those banks will improve because the money is in the population's hands. Many people prefer to save their money in the bank, but fewer people prefer in the houses. Those who want to save the money in property always think, "What if the bank collapses, or there is an incident at the bank? How are we going to get our money back?" Many people do not trust insurance because sometimes it takes too much time for the insurance company to solve the problems. But when it comes to the world financial crisis, those countries lost almost everything in reserve, and the banks crashed. Many people did not know what to do at that moment. When people were saving their money in the banks, they were always increasing, but when the crisis took place, people and the banks lost everything. Even the insurance companies were affected, and the population could not do anything. There might be a chance for people that saved their money in houses because they can start living with their money that they were saving there, and today many people have started thinking about saving money in their houses.

The Oceania continent has multiple cultures, and the economies must be very important for the development of the population. The financial process in Oceania helps maintain the population so that they can cope in every area of their lives. The viewpoints of the governments are to insure that the people can get the help that they need. The governments construct buildings on the continent for the benefit of the population. Australia is a country where multiple cultures recover in many areas of their lives. Everybody who lives in Australia does not expect his life to be affected because of the financial crisis.

The financial crisis took place in Australia when many people did not pay any attention, especially the poor people who had not received the warning. Many of them only realised it when life became harder than before. Even the government in Australia worked very hard to keep the population on its feet. Everybody was affected from the top to the bottom, even the little children: the snacks in school were reduced. The banks had problems in helping the population because the funds were not sufficient to fix people's problems.

The solution can only be found when all the population, including the poor, and all the cultures are conscious about the financial crisis. When everybody is informed about the problem, they will find the solution, those who do not have money. Inside the human consciousness there is an electric brain signal that tells a person about self-defence. I had a cat, and when I was playing with her, every time she defended herself by presenting her claws. She was not strong enough to stop me, but she tried defending herself. This is also true in human beings. The government always has a method to recover the country's debt, but not everywhere has the same situation.

Barret's article stated, "But all of these propitious factors are themselves amenable to policy action. Countries can—and should—choose to build strong economic fundamentals such as sound financial regulation and a strong fiscal position. Countries can build the systems and linkages that give them better advance warning of looming crises" (Barret, 2011: 13).

Many charities or organisations in Australia, both profit and non-profit, needed help from the government. The banks could not help themselves because they were also part of the organisations in Australia that helped the population manage their finances. When the biggest charities are affected financially, what about the smallest financial institutions? Many small charities and organisations used to rely on the bigger organisations because they were businesses that helped the small charities. Australia's government had established the system to sort out the financial problems for the population, especially for the poor people. There is always disaster in Australia because the financial crisis increased the number of unemployed in the country. A multi-culture country is always hard for people to develop quickly in terms of finances, and many governments that lead multi-culture countries work very hard for everybody to be happy. This is true in Australia: the government works to increase the number of jobs, decrease salaries, and increase taxes. All countries are applying the same method. The financial crisis in Australia stops many systems from improvement, and the government has been challenged during the period when everything began to move forward. Australia has been working very hard to build up their finances to cover the crisis, which is a good idea. The bad thing is that the population supports the government financially. The reason why the people have to contribute financially to the government is that every country in the world faces the same situation at the same time, and there is no one that can help others unless they are the multi-billion-dollar countries. The financial crisis came to take money out of the population in Australia, and even the ministers in the government reacted. Australia has the opportunity to recover from the financial crisis because the country has the respect of the other cultures, and these cultures are also human beings who live in Australia.

The American continent resembles many different cultures; most cultures are not originally from America because it is a new continent that has been discovered after Europe, Africa, and Asia. Since the beginning of the continent, people went there to invade for different reasons, and immigration was not hard to do. Before the financial crisis in 2007-2008 took place, American populations were surviving without any conflict in their normal lives, and the government had everything under control. The banks were functioning without any trouble, and when somebody needed to borrow money, the banks had no problem with helping that person. Before the financial crisis, America was supporting many countries, especially poor countries. Many American citizens tried very hard to come out of the financial difficulties in their states by setting up the biggest industries in the world. Many governments were contacting the American government to borrow the money to feed their population, and some of the countries could not survive without America's help. Many people think the United States could not ask for a loan from another country, but after all the financial crises, America was one of the first continents in the world to seek financial help. Perhaps it was because many countries would come seek financial help from them, and the United States needed the provisions. When people came to them, there was no need to explain to people about the financial difficulty, but because they always help people, they will still need to do it until everybody is satisfied. Everybody saw how President Obama struggled very hard to resolve the financial crisis for his population; he was not a perfect person, but he was doing his best. Financial crises destabilised the United States, and some of the population had no idea how they were going to recover from their personal debts. The banks did not have enough financial support to help the public; there was also issues with the insurances companies, and many businesses collapsed at that time.

The article "NBER Working Paper Series Crisis and Responses" states, "In the early stages of the crisis, the situation often arose in which a well-capitalized bank was forced to make sudden large loans based on previously committed lines of credit. In this circumstance, central bank actions can ease liquidity constraints by supplying banks with the funds they need in the short term" (Cecchetti, 2007-2008: 1). When the financial crisis took place in America, the United States set up a system that could help the banks to back up financially, because the government needed the money to manage the continent. The banks should raise their finances in order to help everybody; the banks had a major role to contribute. Most of the population in America relied on the banks because the banks had methods of adding interest to saving accounts. America worked hard to raise jobs for the population to recover, and the government got the financial support to give to the banks. After that, the banks should have a responsibility to manage the financial crisis. In America, everybody started working very hard, and the jobs and hours have been increased. It is because the US government needs to be increased financially. What the United States is doing is using people to increase the money in the bank, but they forgot to make sense of the situation for everybody to have the responsibility to do something. America is a multi-culture continent, and everybody is aware of the United States' financial situation. According to the continent's history, America is a new continent in the world to be discovered. Every American citizen should be aware of the situation that is going on in America and take it into consideration.

One day when I went to buy something in a shop, I was doubting the purchase of that item, and the shop person said to me, "My son, buy it now because you do not what is going to happen to you tomorrow." I think it is the same with visitors in America, as well as people who do not want to consider living in America but are there at the moment. Those people need to contribute for the development of America.

The European continent has multiple cultures, and it has the ideology of colonisation. In other terms, it is the continent that started to discover the rest of the world. Many Europeans think of developing their own countries and being in unity; the euro currency is a symbol of being united rather than each country having its own currency. When Europe had the idea of unity, the countries became more powerful in their economies, and a lot of people were satisfied when they saw the meetings of European authorities. After the First and the Second World Wars, Europeans decided to have peace within their countries and be united. The wars brought disasters into the world, and many European countries were in conflict. The Berlin Wall separated many families, and people could not see each other; peace was restored when the wall was broken. Immigration has been reduced because of the Schengen visa ideology: the Europe gave to many countries within its continent the liberty to travel freely, and there is no trouble when the destination country is inside the Schengen system. All these strategies help Europe grow up financially and in other areas such as technology. People in Europe have the potential to use their currency in many countries without looking for a money exchange bureau. At the time when Europe was making this reconciliation, there were not any bad ideas about the financial crisis; every European was happy to see how Europe was developing at that time. Even the technology started to become one, like the currency system, because somebody could call another person in a different European country free of charge. The communication system became available to any European citizen; people can communicate with each other and share information by using the telephone or other technology systems.

Hodson and Quaglia (2009) stated, "Europe's exposure to the crisis challenges our understanding of the role of banks and financial institutions in European models of capitalism and the complex relationship between economic, monetary and financial integration within the EU" (2009: 950). The financial crisis in Europe challenged the way Europeans think and manage their finances. The financial crisis caused many businesses and companies to collapse; even staff members left jobs because of lack of payment. I went to look for a job in 2008, and they offered me a job but with a condition to accept to work voluntarily; the reason were because the company had lost more than one hundred thousand pounds due to the European financial crisis. I believe that everybody in that company had bills to pay, because the staff were adults but had to work for free. I realised that when I saw one of the managers quit his job and find a job in a restaurant; he had no choice because there was joblessness everywhere at that period. Each person has a bad souvenir from that financial crisis, which took place during 2007-2008. Some people sold their houses, furniture, and all their equipment at cheap prices in order to back up their finances. People were panicking emotionally, especially those who had debts, because in Europe most of the population lived in debt from cars and houses. The government was supposed to work hard to lend the money to banks, and the banks would know how to manage the government financial. Some people complained that even their pets did not have enough food to eat. Many debts were reduced. I remember I had bills to pay to the telephone company, but I told them I had no money to pay them because everybody was struggling very hard, and they understood and gave me more time to pay my bills. The multi-culture continent of Europe struggles to recover from the financial crisis as soon as possible, because many countries from Africa borrow money from Europe. Europe decreased tax and did many other things so that people would be able to pay, and it kept the continent financially stable. Every citizen in the Europe continent has the right to have enough money to survive, and this is why it is the governments' duty to help the population.

b) Affected Areas

The Affected areas can be identified in many ways. In this book I selected particular areas to discuss the essentials points, which can give each individual an understanding of the problems and solutions. When there is a problem in the world, there will be always the main areas that many people expect to hear about, because these are the most impressive places or people. In a human being's life, there is always upper class and lower class, and there is no need to change this system because it is supposed to be this way. As I've always said, people do not chose their families or places to be born, because if there was a choice, the royal families would be packed. Nobody would want to be born into poor places or families.

Regardless, we need to deal with the families and places where we were born. There are the main countries that have been affected, because many countries seek the help from them; for example, many African countries seek help from European countries and the United States. Nobody can deny how those countries are helping each other and solving many problems in different countries, and the leaders of the countries are the eyewitnesses of those countries. There are also governments that are tremendously affected due to the financial crisis; those governments had to work very hard to recover in order to find the solution for their own countries and for the rest of the countries around the world.

In politics there are always many issues that have been affected. Politics is the main system that drives an entire country and its population. Social life is affected because there also many cultural problems that need a solution. Finally, the religion is also a major area of human life that can be affected in a financial crisis, because many people are religious, and leaders support the religious group that is most popular in their countries.

i) Countries

Many countries today have been affected, and it will take generations to resolve because it is the first massive world economy crisis. The European countries have been affected by the financial crisis since 2007; many people lost their jobs, and families have been seriously affected. The incident happed consciously in people's minds, and many people in Europe now do not know how it happened. The economy crisis attacked every citizen who lived in Europe at that time. The financial crisis traumatised certain people in the UK more than the Second World War. The UK banks lost money, businesses collapsed, and charity organisations that depended on the government could not recover. Many marriages ended because of financial difficulty, and people did not know how to resolve family matters. The problems increased without any solution in sight. I believe that the number of deaths increased in the world, especially the number of heart attacks. Most businesses shut down completely, and the owners of the businesses could not cope or recover financially. Employees of those businesses became jobless, and those with large families had serious problems in managing their families. Christmas in those years was not impacted because many people in UK reduced their spending to save for Christmas gifts. For those who prefer to travel for Christmas, I think there was some reconsideration in those times because people prefer not to spend too much when they lack money. In London there is always the weekend market, where they sell second-hand items at lower prices. When I visited there, I asked somebody why they were selling their furniture, and he answered that he needed the money because of the financial crisis. I saw many people who had never been to that market sell their equipment at low prices just to get something to eat.

In the article "UK financial crisis 'as serious as a war'", The Journal stated, "The economic impact of the global financial crisis has been as devastating as a world war, a senior Bank of England official said yesterday. Andy Haldane, the Bank's executive director for financial stability, said that public anger at the banks was fully justified" (2009).

The financial crisis was affected more people than a war. One of the bank's staff said that the population was uncomfortable financially. People's expenses were tremendously affected; even the last two World Wars did not achieve a financial crisis like this. The bank staff mentioned that the repayment for covering these debts would still be taking place three generations from 2007. The population had a right to be anxious because they had lost their fortunes, and no one in the country could help each other because the incidents attacked the entire world. The banks should allow businesses to borrow money for recouping what they lost. Some of the customers usually kept their money in banks, and whenever banks collapse, it is very hard for the customers to accept apologies from the banks. The banks lost their customers' confidence because these people would not trust banks again.

Businesses reduced people's salaries in order to recover from the financial crisis in UK, but the council tax bills were not reduced in that moment. The UK population would be dealing with this issue for years, waiting for the solution to come. Mortgages have been hindering many people, and some sold their properties to recover financially. The most dangerous things are the mortgages offered by the banks, because many people visit the banks to get the mortgages and loans for houses and flats. In this case there has been chaos, and in many cases some people cannot cope and recover from this incident. The UK banks need the people to put confidence in them. Now the population has the advantage to choose which UK bank can cover the insurance after the financial crisis.

Europe has increased its taxes due to the financial crisis, and one of the reasons is to back up certain banks and solve the people's problems as a temporary solution, especially in France. The European continent helps many countries, as I said previously in this book. When countries such as France are in crisis, it means certain countries that depend on France's economy also face serious financial problems. The financial crisis affected France in many areas. The multi-culture countries need to work rapidly on their economics and sort out businesses. France is a multi-culture country because a lot of the population comes from West Africa: Morocco, Algeria, Tunisia, Libya, and Egypt. As everybody knows, those countries are based on the Arabian system, and Islam is the most common religion for them. France was based on Christianity, but now Islam is becoming more popular. When the financial crisis attacked the country, it is not just the French people who were affected, but it was also the other cultures in France.

Many businesses were affected by the financial crisis in France, and the trust of the banks were reduced because everybody was scared to keep the money in banks. The banks should work out how they can bring back their customers. To bring the customers back, banks didn't give them money for free, but they showed them their efficiency. The banks improved their systems even in the financial crisis; they reacted as quickly as possible before their customers decided to leave them. In a country where there are multiple cultures, it has always been very hard to control everybody at the same time. Before making the decision, you have to look at other cultures' reactions and analyse their ways of thinking, because they are also part of the population and can contribute to many things in the country. There is no need to condemn the other cultures in the country or consider them only when the country urgently needs something.

Schubert stated, "'A tax increase of 80 percent. Such a thing doesn't exist even in North Korea,' complained Jean-David Chamboredon, one of the co-founders of The Pigeons initiative and head of Isai, an investment company. How can start-ups find the necessary private investors—'business angels', as the French call them, too—when they are faced with not only the high risk of such investments, but now also such government theft?" (Hollande Makes a Start, 2013). Due to financial crisis, French investors did not understand the reaction of the government because they'd never seen such a disaster before. Before, France appreciated the work of its investors because they were helping the French banks, but it would be not easy for these investors to do their business as usual because of the financial crisis. The French government worked very hard to help those investors keep going on as normal business, but there would still be struggles because the benefits and profits would not be enough. The French tried to offer to the investors more profit, but there was not enough for the investors to accept, because most of them did not want to lose anything when they did their business. The investors would not accept the offer from the France, and in the meantime France would still have the problem to solve regarding the banks and the French people. The situation in France was much better before, but politics and businesses started to get involved because another president took over, and the president who was leaving decided to cancel many sources because they reduced the percentage of investors in France. When the governments were playing their games, they forgot to think of the civilians in the country, because the people are the ones who suffer, especially the poor populations. The leaders should do the right things for the sake of the population rather than mixing their personal issues with people's lives. It is not just one generation affected—three generations will be affected in France. Everybody in France has the right to live democratically, and this is not the time to ask for each individual's opinion, but compassion and love of the country should be promoted. France's leaders have a duty to consider their people first rather than looking into conflict politics.

America is the continent that usually helps the most countries in the world. Most countries have developed because of the United States, and the constitutions of those countries have become stable because of America. Before the financial crisis, the United States was developing day after day without any problems, and US citizens were surviving peacefully. Financially the United States had no problems because nobody was affected financially, not even the poor people who do not work. The leaders were in control of everything because the finances were available before the world economic crisis. The government was able to feed many countries and their own population.

In the time of the financial crisis, many people became uncomfortable and emotional, and many people suffered heart attacks because the banks crashed. The governments organised several meetings to meet the criteria of the financial problem, but nothing was improved. One of the reasons was because the United States was responsible for many countries in the world and supported those countries financially. The US government invited many organisations to the meeting to sort out the financial issues, because a solution was needed at that moment to recover their population and other countries around the world. Many of the meetings were about solving the debts in the United States: the amount of debts were still increasing, and even the government stopped functioning. The US population became in debt, until they decided to be in debt to different countries in order to solve their population. The leaders decided to resolve the financial crisis because there was no choice, and they couldn't deny the failure that had occurred. But there was a chance for the United States to seek help from the countries whom they were helping.

Even America was making a lot of effort, but there was still a need for the help of every country that had financial potential to help the world. Every big organisation in the world should have done something to reach a solution about the financial crisis. The decision from many countries was based on taxes. Increasing taxes in the world was not the right decision for people who could not afford it. The world was not made to have a financial crisis. We have been recovering for many years, and no organisations are giving a good explanation about the true cause of the financial crisis. I always stand at the back of the audience to hear if the sound can reach people seated in the back. In other words, what about the people that live somewhere outside the big organisations? They are considered or made aware of the situation. According to Labaton and Zeleny, "But with the markets slowly healing, Mr. Obama's plan to revamp financial rules faces a diminishing political imperative. Disenchantment by many Americans with big government, along with growing obstacles from financial industry lobbyists pressing Congress not to do anything drastic, have also helped to stall his proposals" (For Obama, a Chance to Reform the Street Is Fading, 2009). It was not bad to look for the solution at that stage, because it was legal for the world to challenge human beings, and everybody felt something was not right in the world. They should invite those big organisations to seek the solution, because those organisations have a sense of that crisis. Also, in many countries the investors tracked many countries by asking the government to reduce taxes when the government was looking for help to recover from the financial crisis.

The financial situation in the United States started to improve gradually in 2009. President Obama made the decision to reduce pressure from politics because he had to improve on certain decisions that several businesses suggested. In this problem, there is no need to wait for the politicians to decide, because most of the investors are not interested in politics, thought there might interest in political sponsorship. Everybody expected to hear the understanding of the US president about the financial crisis, but the problem struck everybody in the world, especially new presidents who had just come to power. The logic of the situation is that the new president who came across the incident of the financial crisis had something new to restore the financial needs of the population, because all of the population relies on the president. The financial crisis disappointed many people's celebrations and special occasions; some people had their anniversaries in those periods, and they had to cancel because of the financial problem. My suggestion was that if they cancelled their events, it would not change anything and would only make them feel bad. They could reduce the celebration expenses. The speech of President Obama was based on negative criticism because he suggested that the solution to the financial crisis concerned everybody in the nation, and the choice should be fit for every US citizen. The solution of the United States had to look towards future generations because it was important to focus on that generation rather than running in a circle without finding potential solutions. Psychologically, US citizens should analyse how to develop the financial situations that invaded their nation without warning, because almost the entire population was not aware of the financial crisis. If the people were aware, they would get their money from the banks, and most of the investors would keep their money in cash. The US population should check all areas of their lives in order to make the decision; otherwise the situation might be worse in the future.

If the United States did not announce the financial crisis, maybe not everybody would realise the issue, and people would live normal lives. Perhaps some people would feel the prices of the foods had increased, certain people would lose their jobs. Some people lived in villages where technology couldn't reach them to confirm the financial failure; those people did not feel anything strange. I met people in those villages, and they did not even consider whether there was electricity for lights; for them, lights were not a part of their lives. Those people do not even know about their presidents—they aren't even interested in the politics of their countries. I interviewed a man and asked if he wanted to become president. He answered that it was not his job to become president, because he was not even interested in it.

It was not a bad idea to reassemble the leaders for the solution, because logically everybody who knew about the financial crisis was interested in a solution as soon as possible. Many people suffered emotionally because the news of the financial crisis kept the world hostage. When somebody does not know she has cancer, that person will feel fine. But after a test result of cancer, the same person will start to suffer emotionally. According to Lowrey and Popper, "The leaders came to Washington to talk about the international recovery, Ms. Lagarde said in an interview on the NBC News program *Meet the Press*. 'Then they found out that the debt ceiling was the issue,' she added. 'They found out that the government had shut down and that there was no remedy in sight.' 'So it really completely transformed the meeting in the last few days,' Ms. Lagarde said" (World Leaders Press the US on Fiscal Crisis, 2013). The impression of the meeting was good. The solution took very long to arrive because the investors did not want to give a chance to the government, and the government acted in the same manner.

There were various sorts of meetings for financial recovery in the United States, and several organisations decided to come together to discuss about the solution and find out how to heal the symptoms of the financial crisis. Things go better when there is a problem that the major organisations need to resolve together, and this was what the most US organisations did. Even the government did not have the potential to function, but after the biggest organisations came together, there was again confidence in the government. The government felt better and could deal with the financial issues for the people to recover more than before, because most of the countries in the world relied on the US government. Several organisations in

America helped the government not to be overwhelmed with the pressure, and that led them to the high risk of debts in the United States. The US government should keep its promises to its people— it could be dangerous if the solution does not come quickly, because it would cause a disaster in numerous US families. Most of the families in the United States work full-time jobs and pay bills and taxes regularly. With the financial crisis, it could be harder for some people to cope with these difficulties. The United States suggested that if the organisations could not come together, there would be financial borrowing everywhere in America. The world economy could not support the weight of the borrowing in the world, and the entire world would be concerned with their governments. The meeting globalised the ideas from many organisations, and they realised that some of the banks could stop working due to the financial crisis—and the consequence could be dreadful. Also, several businesses were not functioning. During the meeting, the organisation realised the United States had a responsibility to the world, and investors should help in the global financial crisis. The US banks had to work together with potential investors to recover from the financial crisis, and that should benefit everyone on the planet.

The entire world has never been happy for a few second. The leaders of the world have their own problems, and their private lives need solutions as well. The solution of the world will not just come from small groups of leaders; there are also other leaders in the world that many constitutions ignore. Having a solution for the war on finance by a few leaders is not a bad impression, as far as democracy is concerned. Without a solution on the financial crisis, many countries in the world would have serious money scares, and lots of families will be affected. In most countries if the solution did come quickly, many parents would not support their children for a long period of time, and they would ask their children to go out and look for money. The world should be very careful not to waste many souls due to a scarcity of finances and food. Nobody deserves to live without finances, and everybody needs financial help. I wonder whether some children know about real money when somebody gives them a choice. According to

Lowrey and Popper, "Many of the high-ranking officials present in Washington for the meetings made open appeals to Congress, with warnings coming from many of Washington's allies and creditors. Ms. Lagarde's counterpart at the World Bank, the American physician Jim Yong Kim, said the world was "days away from a very dangerous moment" (World Leaders Press the US on Fiscal Crisis, 2013). The solution is always appreciated because it brings happiness to everybody, and many people enjoy having a solution to their problems. Everybody has a duty to find the solution to the financial crisis, even a person who does not work. In the poorest countries, some hear about the noise because a human being is an agent; that is, if somebody is not happy, it means another person is also not happy.

With a lack of confidence in the United States, several countries' economies would crash, especially the countries that rely on America. The US economy influences numerous countries in the world. Even in Europe, countries were pressuring the United States to be reliable again as quickly as possible, because the entire world was waiting for America's reaction. The US decisions and solutions were for that moment only—but what about future problems? The United States also had to think about future financial crises because as long as the world exists, the problems will still come, though perhaps in different way. America should think about how to control the problems that come for the next generations, because in the previous generations there were bloody wars, but 2007-2008 was the financial war. In order to get solutions from the different types of people, everybody's idea of contribution is important, because one person cannot decide in the place of many people. The contribution of scientists, politicians, and other organisations are always important for the development of the solution. The United States ensures that whenever they unite together with different sorts of organisations, the solutions will be taken into consideration, and everything is agreed with the spirit of unification, taken into consideration without judgement. Many people were satisfied to see how the financial war crisis was settling down, and the nation decided to exterminate that danger. Everybody was affected, and the governments had no power to help. The solution came when the organisations and other groups decided to be united. Even the US military forces gave their ideas in the meeting.

ii) Government and Politics

As I described before about the financial crisis, with all the analyses and other issues, there will always be difficulties for future generations because countries' populations are still growing in number. The solution could be taken to temporarily resolve the problems, but it's not permanent. People the right to seek loans in many places, because the situation of the government was very critical. This solution will not be for the people to be fully recovered, but it will let people understand the economy failure in the world; there will never be a final solution. The solution could not be found at that moment when many investors came together.

One of the aspects that can prevent the solution from coming as quickly as possible is because the financial crisis took place across the entire world. The government would have the serious misgivings about other countries politically and financially. The war on financial crisis raised several issues around the world, and many people have financial problems that need to be solved. If the big countries have a problem finding the solution, what about the countries that rely on them? The imperative suggestion is that if the biggest countries that help other countries need the high risk of borrowing, then the smallest countries need less borrowing. The more problems that the biggest countries have, the fewer problems that will be in the smallest countries. When you look into the specific problem in each country, there are several problems in each of them that arose at that time, and their populations were affected.

Zingales stated, "That, unfortunately, is the story of the American authorities' intervention during the 2008 financial crisis. After the collapse of Bear Stearns, it was clear that more problems were coming, yet the United States government did nothing. In July 2008, when

Fannie Mae and Freddie Mac (the government-backed housing-loan agencies) were found to be insolvent, then Treasury Secretary Hank Paulson promised a 'bazooka,' but delivered what turned out to be a slingshot. It was only after Lehman Brothers collapsed that Paulson went to Congress seeking $700 billion to stabilize the financial system" (*Social Europe Journal,* 2011). The US financial crisis carried the destruction US populations, and many Americans could not find positive results. The involvement of other organisations failed to help the war on the financial crisis. There was still tragedy in the future of the US government because the solution was found in the first financial crisis. The government was in charge to resolve many problems because most of the people relied on the government. Even when they organised together to find the solution, the solution did not meet all the criteria to cover the financial crisis. Many people did not have the ability to get accommodations easily, and the government realised that the numbers of homeless would increase in number. They decided to help the population with housing options. It is always exceptional to have somewhere to live and sleep, rather than having food without a house. According to the political meeting, the decision was made that the US government had to raise millions of dollars to support the country. The suggestion was not easy because in that period all the world had the same suffering and was seeking financial help. Many governments in the world were in search of financial help to cover the finances for their countries. The politicians had to change their ways of governance because they could not function with low budgets; they needed financial help, and none of the governments in that period were strong financially. Any financial help was hard to find, but it was very helpful to the US government because they were eager financially. The United States was increasing in debt to other countries because the government was borrowing everywhere, and that debt would cause lots of debts in the future. In the future the US government must work very hard to prevent a financial crisis and to protect the country from being in debt to others. The American people have to work hard to help their government financially.

The political intervention in the financial crisis was resolved. In the world, politician is always after certain power or leadership. Other politicians will be in opposition, not just to help the ones in power but to stop them from progressing. That way the population will become angry at the political party leading at that moment. In every war, many politicians have had the ability to analyse problems for the interests of their politic parties, rather than looking for solutions for the entire nation. The same politicians who work for the government for the sake of the people use methods that cannot satisfy to the population, because there is always the opposition party that will never commit to the other side's decisions. If politicians should come without a opposition party, or the opposition had a conscience to accept the principles of the party leading at the moment, the population would be satisfied. There is always the possibility for the entire politician to come with a positive idea to help each other for the development of the country. In France, when President Nicola Sarkozy lost the election, France's financial situation was wobbling because many organisations were helping his political party to work accurately. The new president that came at time struggled too much and resemble the African countries in its need for financial help.

Africa needed the development of human rights because it is a young continent in human rights and democracy. By the time the entire African continent has the ability to apply for right humans and democracy, they will not need help from Western countries because they will be in charge of doing everything. The way that African politicians currently lead their countries, it seems that they do not really like their own countries as much as Western politicians like their Western populations.

Zingales stated, "Second, there is no political reward for fighting a preventive war, while there is great political capital to be earned by acting after problems have exploded. Had Franklin Roosevelt succeeded in preventing the Pearl Harbor attack with a pre-emptive strike against Japan, we would still be discussing whether war with Japan was inevitable. Roosevelt waited to act until after the catastrophe, and he has been revered as a savior. To act, politicians need consensus, which often does not emerge until the costs of inaction have become highly visible. By that point, it is often too late to avoid a much worse outcome" (*Social Europe Journal,* 2011). None of the politicians used to feel comfortable when they did something that was convenient for their people. In the world today, a politician defends the country for the sake of his own principles, and especially for his own interests. In many wars throughout the world, the political parties play many roles in terms of finding the solution, because politics is always a main system in the world that manipulates the population. As I mentioned before, people do not want to die in the world, and they believe that politicians are also human beings and should think the same way as the public. Politicians have the same feelings as other people; they are part of our families and could be some our sisters and brothers and neighbours. Before many people start thinking politics, they think on the terminology of politics because the political parties are also based on principles. A political party resembles many different sorts of people with the different understandings. The result of a political strategy is always capable of functioning in order to satisfy people's needs, because political parties are the solution to the population. There is also confidentiality within most politics parties.

The negative side of the political party is when there is disagreement. Disputes occur with other political parties; people who are not into politics find it very frustrating when politicians oppose each other. Politics always has at least two strategies and ideologies, which is very fundamental because the politicians help the populations when they are in need. Politicians always show their ability to do good jobs, and the negativity is that when the politicians already had the opportunity to lead a particular group and did not keep their promises. The people are suffering too much in these nations; if people should have freedom of speech, then the politicians should understand their needs. I think the world will change as quickly as it can.

Many people lost jobs during the financial crisis. When people lost jobs, the governments should have decreased taxes rather than increase them. But the governments ignored the common people, because the politicians' analyses indicated that by increasing taxes, the country might recover quicker. That analysis was the weapon to hijack the people financially. Politicians only analyse how they can win elections. The results of the politician's party politics is always different than the population's; before the election, politicians are similar to the population, but after the election the politicians always change their policies. A lot of governments in many countries cannot find the solution for the financial crisis because the political aspect of leading is not satisfied.

The deontology of the government is always different than politics, but they are in the same system when it comes to leadership. I knew somebody who worked for the government for many years, but he worked with the different presidents and ministers. Every time he told me that he did not have any responsibility to change a law in that country, because it was the politicians' duty to change the laws. I began to understand how politics control the government institution: the government must take into consideration anything that the politicians say. When the biggest institution cannot resolve the problem on the financial crisis—because looking for the solution would lead them to manipulate the smallest countries in the world into finding the solution—then in order to look for the solution, one would lead people to react without the consideration of the law. Politics control the world economy, but when it comes to the war on the financial crisis, the government works hard to recover many debts, including the political parties' debts. But it is always politics that causes many incidents in the world.

The governments around the world, especially the countries that are involved in sorting out the financial crisis, should stand together and respect the role of government. The government is an institution that interprets what the president or queen decides, and not what the investors suggest. The population that lives in the country does not have the right to challenge it, even if there is freedom of speech; the government should act as the dictator to lead the population. The war on the financial crisis challenged the governments, but the governments were blind to realise that the investors are also the people that live in the country. Even with the rise of unemployed, the investors would challenge the governments to reduce taxes, but the governments increased taxes instead. Ali Kabasakal Görmüş said, 'Brender and Drazen claimed that positive economic growth decreases unemployment and improves government services through increase in government revenue. Their empirical study investigates the effect of macroeconomic variables on re-election of incumbent government for a sample of 74 countries over the period of 1960-2003 using discrete choice model" (2010). The institutions across the world have been infected due to the war on the financial crisis. The number of political parties were reduced in order to keep the top parties going. Most of the governments in the world dealt with businessmen to back them up, and the governments in their turn should have the ability to help the businessmen—not because they helped them, but because they are citizens of the country. When there is a strike in a particular incident, everybody should be considered because everybody has a talent to contribute. In politics there is always a sacrifice because it is always the politician's duty to make the people rich. However, the politicians often become more rich than the population.

The governments used the population's finances to cover the financial crisis. People started to struggle for jobs, and the governments should apply a good method to take the money out of the population, but most of the governments did not have a good ideology. Therefore the re-election probability of incumbent governments may increase. Many governments in the world observe their finances in order to organise and be ready for elections in their countries. The acceptable ideas that were used in the past did not impact the financial crisis. The financial crisis affected elections, and many of the elections were cancelled because the government could not provide the finances to the public. In the countries where funds were very difficult to find, the governments decided to prevent many political parties from joining the elections, and those politics parties had to do something else or else wait for the next election. After many tests by different organisations, there was always the result of politics failing in many countries. The political parties were responsible for the financial crisis; the population had nothing to do with the failure of the finance crisis. But after the war on the financial crisis, there is a troubled psychology between the citizens and the governments. The governments rely on politics because most of the politicians occupy the biggest position in the government. The governments do not have policies that can prevent politicians from controlling them, because most of the members in political parties work in the government to affect the government and make it choose their policies, which help them to keep leading. For this reason there will be always and chaos in the world, especially in the poorest countries where money is scarce. The populations will not cope with the conditions. The financial crisis prevents many political parties from solving problems.

The financial crisis brought the world's food prices to expensive levels because many people lost the ability to manage their food in their communities. People suffered badly in the countries with food crises. In South Africa, they discovered many cows were dying because they were eating certain grasses. Those grasses could not produce the proper vitamins—they produced poison instead. The food crisis caused a lot of disaster in the world because all living creatures require food to eat, and without food the populations cannot live in good conditions. When there is a financial crisis, the farmers suffer regarding the development of their businesses, because the populations are unable to purchase their foods. In the countries where money was scarce, there would be a problem with transportation because most of the farmers were in the countryside. In most countries when there is a financial difficulty, people do not have the ability to reach the countryside. The populations were unable to control their food prices, and sometimes businesses increased the prices because the owners knew about the financial crisis.

In countries where democracies were not in place, the population had no right to say anything to their governments. The war on the financial crisis was traumatic, and the lives of many people were affected because they lost their jobs. The governments with their political business had a duty to control the prices of food during the financial crisis, rather than increase the prices. Lagi, Bertrand, and Bar-Yam stated, "Food price controls in the face of high global food prices carry associated costs. Because of the strong cascade of events in the Middle East and North Africa only some countries had to fail to adequately control food prices for events to unfold" (2011).

The importance of the food prices is for social stability. The analysis presented of the timing of peaks in global food prices and social unrest implies that the 2011 unrest was precipitated by a food crisis that threatened the security of vulnerable populations. The governments of the world did help the population because most people did not have good jobs, and others' jobs were suspended, but those who were jobless could afford to buy food. The population could not be as secured as before the food prices rose in all the nations; the politicians should have the ability to discuss the prices of the foods. Many people in the nations condemned the ways in which the governments and politicians were acting towards their own populations. Many organisations in the world organised campaigns that could help reduce food costs for the populations to recover. The political parties that were also against putting too much pressure on the government were leading the countries, and it happened to many countries, but the politics parties in power did not impact their citizens. The population became very unfaithful to their leaders, and the leaders had to have the abilities to prepare for good governance in the years to come, or else they would lose their countries. The next political parties that came to power to lead the countries had to set in motion good policies so that they could also work out for the next generation.

Many governments in the world have duties to consider, such as the price of food for the population, because food has an important role to play among people. When foods are at high prices, what about when somebody is sick in the hospital? Most of the medications that people take require food in the body, for good energy. When some of the population begin to rise up, they express their opposition to their leaders. The world governments from 2007 should react as quickly as possible to control the world markets' regulation in order to be affect the consciousness of their populations. The duties of the politicians should be to respect human rights, and the health of the population need to be treated with priority.

The lives of many people have been affected because of social crises and religious crises. Leaders have suffered to recover stability within religions, because religion has a major role in society. Religion is the second place to discover the social lives of the people in these nations. When people are gathering together to express their emotions and feelings, it is very efficient, but when the financial disaster comes to tackle them, many people are unable to recover. The help of religion allows many people to express their opinions in public. Religion can also be identified as the voice of the people who do not have voices. When there is a problem in the community or a family, many people can take refuge in a religious group to find the solutions of their problems. Many organisations use religion as a mediator for their solutions, but when there is a crisis in the group's religion, the people do not find a solution. Even the governments around the world consider religion as the second institution in the country, because most of the people in the world belong to a religion. All the queens, kings, presidents, and ministers, have also their own religion preferences, and their consciences have developed a particular way because of it.

In a crisis, many people will be disqualified to honour their own religions; nobody wants to see her traditional religions fall. If the people are supposed to live together and express their feelings, their concerns should be explored. Politicians will create strategies to cause disorder in the religious groups, to separate people who have been living together for several years. The politicians who are already members of a certain religious group need to analyse the rights of the religion in the government. When the world is changing in many different ways, it is not necessary to dismiss religion; all organisations have a right to contribute to any situation.

The issue of religion is always about the individual understanding the elements that are located in the principles of the religion. Many believers follow what their leaders tell them to do, but the believers may forget their duties within the group. The believers have choices to make when their leaders are not leading them in an appropriate way. I have written a book titled *African Inter-Religious: Philosophy and Theology*, and in this book I made many comments about the African religions and why Africans leave their traditional religions and join Western religions. The incident caused by two religions in African is not something that can be stopped easily and quickly. Christianity and Islam are the same religion but do not have the same philosophy background; also, the way of teaching those religions in Africa is totally different. In Africa they are both condemned on many points. David Smith of Okapi Consulting stated, "'Signs of hope: Is it too late to make sense of what is happening in the Central African Republic? A Muslim neighbour helped me reach this camp when I was trying to escape the fighting"—Christine, a Christian woman in Bossangoa" (*BBC Africa News,* 13 December 2013). The African ancestors did not know anything about Islam or Christianity, but they were living life abundantly, and now there is killing amongst themselves because of those two religions. The ancestors had religions which they thought were the true God, but there was no taking them into consideration because the postcolonial missionaries presented them with different religions. The cause of this war in Central Africa is because of the Western religions, not African traditional religions. Those two cannot ever become traditional African religions because African have their own religions from their ancestors; they may ignore them, but they are still in their blood.

There is a question to ask: why are there are always disasters in other countries? If a peace is found in one country, then there will be a disaster in a different country. The world never has full peace for a second—there is always disorder somewhere in the world, and human beings cannot live with a peace any more. The religious wars are always disastrous because they spill innocent blood without a good reason; it ends with the eternal conflict, and people's social lives will not be confident. Many people have doubt because in certain countries there will not be a religious peace due to past religious wars. The population will be left with individual conflicts from one generation to another. When there are two different religious groups within the family, that family will not remain stable because of past conflict. In the same situation, there will not be two different neighbours with different religious groups living in the same neighbourhood. When a couple does not have the same religion, the marriage will be very difficult, and the religion and social crises cause fear within lots of families. Everybody that belongs to a different religious group wears different clothes, but in countries where there is a conflict between those religious group, the populations will not live comfortably. Even that Christian woman had help from a Muslim neighbour. The solution had been found, but she would be still frightened by Muslim citizens.

The crisis created problems which many people did not expect to see at that moment, because they used to live together with their fellow Muslims. Regret was left in many people's hearts because their friendships with other religious groups had been lost, and the religious crisis prevented them from living in harmony. The incidents happened because history repeats itself, and there was already the same system of war but in a different way; the previous problems were about rebellious troops. After that, there was unacceptable occasion that challenged many social aspects of the population. The rebellious war changed to a religious rebellious war in the country, and the religious leaders in that country should have had the authority to confront politicians about the crisis. The religions in Central African Republic do not communicate with each other regarding the well-being of the public. For more on this, you can read my book *African Inter-Religious: Philosophy and Theology*.

Many countries were led by one president only, and the identity of that president was also important so that people could see him in at a temple. People who have the same religion as the president will be proud. Some of the people who do not have the same religious groups as their leaders do not have the right to express their opinions in that country, especially in a country that is led by a dictator. In Africa there are two major religious groups which most of the population follow, and in these religions most people respect the way that the world functions. Africa's system of success used to be taken into consideration, but sometimes when the leader belongs to a particular ethnic group or religion, that leader will help only the people who come from the same group.

Many people rely on politicians in Africa; Africans prefer to become politicians rather than look for other ways to help people. Many countries in Africa have angry populations. There are always misunderstandings when politics play the role of encouraging a feeble group, but the government has a duty to help the people who do not have power. The incident of Central Africa showed us that everybody was supporting the Christian religion rather than Islam. One of the reasons was that the populations have a Christian background. Islam was not taken into consideration in Central Africa; this was established by the missionaries, and most of the missionaries who went to Central Africa were Christian. The religious crisis brought bad memories to the people of Central Africa, and many people's social lives were affected because of the war. It also happened roughly six years after financial crisis, when everybody was trying very hard to find solutions. Many people from different countries sometimes have problems that cannot be improved without the help of other countries.

The missionaries invaded Africa for many reasons. In everything that human beings do, there are always bad and good reasons, but it is always better to accept the good points and to keep good friendships going. The situation that happened in Central Africa is one of many reasons that I have analysed the situation. We should ask ourselves when that problem started. The people of Central Africa had the right to fight against bad governance because the country did not have enough finances to support itself; it is one the poorest countries in the world. The government of Central Africa has a duty to control the territory of the country and secure the people with a stability of life, because the government is in service of the population. Many people from the corners of Central Africa have the freedom to live good lives.

These types of conflicts happen in many countries in Africa. In Europe it is very rare to see the fighting and conflicts involving religions. When there is conflict between religious groups, one of the reasons is that those religions are massive in numbers, and none of the leaders will let another leader from a different religious group control and lead his own group. It is very difficult for leaders to let other religious leaders give instruction to them, because many of the leaders in Africa want to be known and like it when people cheer for them. The religious crisis is always the biggest conflict in the world, and it affects the entire social life across the world; even when it happens to one country, the rest of the countries will be also affected. Many people that belong to that particular religious group will be against people that belong to another group. Similar incidents happened in other countries, especially in Africa. Africa is a young continent in the exporting of religious groups because most of religions which the Africans practice are imports.

Christianity took hold in the period of colonisation all over the Africa continent, particularly in West Africa. The majority of the African peoples prefer to be Christians by birth, and social life is based on Christianity ideology. Most of the leaders in Africa encourage Christianity rather than other religious groups. Most Christian missionaries use many strategies to get Africans into their religion. Many of the Christians in African believe in Western Christianity. The West uses many ideas on to get Africans to join their denominations, rather than letting them make their choices with the spirit of democracy in mind. The missionaries expend a lot of energy to have more followers from different countries; it is not a bad idea, but it results in bloodshed for innocent African people.

There is a religious group and social crisis because many African countries were invaded by strong Christianity missionaries, and today the result of the missionaries and their mistakes are now apparent. In some African countries, Christian groups have no impact because they were in the majority. The Christian missionaries preferred to move to other parts of Africa, excluding the north-west and the east, where Islam held the majority. There were always problems before Christianity settled in Africa, but the missionaries use the political system to silence Islam in many countries. It is also the Islamic religious denominations that prevent missionaries from installing Christianity in ai region. For that reason, the missionaries used another weapon to destabilise the mentalities of African people, by teaching them some bad things about the Islam. In every religious group there are always bad and good things, because of the presence of human beings. In a group of people there could be a good character, but there could also be a bad character. Due to their failure in north-east Africa, Christian missionaries pushed to accuse Islam of bad things, creating eternal conflict between families.

Falola argued that "during the nineteenth century, many missionaries had hoped to add the north to the Christian kingdom, but only a few dedicated missionaries could silence Islam. Many were already conditioned to think that Christianity was superior to Islam. In addition, some missionaries went to the extent of thinking that the Islamic religion was a creation of the evil, one that was incapable of bringing liberty, justice, and freedom to humankind" (Falola, 1998: 33-34). The war on religious crisis had not appeared at this time, but it was already planned after the arrival of missionaries in Africa. There was always conflict in the Westerners' plans; it was not to challenge Africa to another traditional religious group, and they needed Africans to follow only Christianity. Many wars started due to religion, and the incident of the Central African population showed many things because they manifested what the missionaries left to them. What if the missionaries taught them that Islam was a good religion? Then Christianity would not create disorder, and there would be peace. There will still be a crisis if all the religions in Africa do not want to reconcile and oppose each other. When a Muslim man became president in Central Africa, the Christians became upset. The government did not have the power to control the religions, and so it asked for help from France's government. The same thing will happen when they choose a Christian to become president: the Muslims will oppose the Christians. The religious crisis will keep going, over and over across the continents.

The world needs to find a solution. There are two major religions that impact the world because they are the most popular. Many wars in the world are caused by these two religious groups, and the world needs to analyse the internal problems. The characteristics of human beings are always different, and there will never be two different people with the same ideas. The solution of the religious crisis is located within their beliefs; believers know their weaknesses and strong points. The religious leaders have to discuss the major problems s occurring within their religions. The social life of the civilians in Central Africa are affected because the religions are not stable—the religions brought the disorder to families, and the population cannot find an appropriate solution.

The religious crisis should be taken into consideration for preventing social life from being adequate; the crisis would have destroyed the lives of many people around the world. Many people in modern times prefer to be well organised within their neighbourhoods because of the security it offers. Neighbours are always the first person to bring security to somebody who is in the danger. The religion should be the solution of the people; when everybody belongs to a particular religion, it means that the solutions must be available the right way. The religious crisis is always relative because many people do not know about what exactly is going on. People should be aware of everything that is going on in their countries. Politics should be more reliable with the population's religious groups.

Religious war has never been understood, and it looks like it is caused by the religious groups themselves, but it is always the business of politicians that manipulate the people who voted for them. Social life is very important, and when a particular political party is taking care of everybody, especially the younger generations, it has to be able to understand the people's history. The citizens have the right to discipline themselves in order to construct a better future for the generations to come. The government should not support only one religion because other denominations can provide contributions. The justice of every country needs to be accurate and reliable in order for the people who live in that country to feel confident with their neighbourhoods. When social life is affected, the people are also affected, and even the politicians will not focus for the development of the country. There is a need for dialogue between religions in order to avoid conflict, and to avoid the failure of the government.

BIBLIOGRAPHY

Australian government, *People, Culture, and Lifestyle.* Available at: http://www.dfat.gov.au/facts/people_culture.html, visited: 31/10/2013 (2012).

Avruch, K., *Culture and Conflict Resolution.* Washington: Endowment of the United States Institute of Peace (1998).

Barrett, C., "Australia and the Great Recession: Per Capita Research Paper". Australia: Per Capita Australia Limited (2011).

BBC News., "BBC On This Day, 1945: It Was Just against Humanity". Available at: http://news.bbc.co.uk/onthisday/hi/witness/august/9/newsid_4720000/4720807.stm, visited: 04/11/2013 (1950-2005).

—"Ex-President Jean-Bedel Bokassa Rehabilitated". Available at: http://www.bbc.co.uk/news/world-africa-11890278, visited: 24/11/2013 (2010).

Cecchetti, S. G., "NBER Working Paper Series Crisis and Responses: The Federal Reserve and the Financial Crisis of 2007-2008". Cambridge: NBER Working Paper No. 14134 (2007-2008).

Davis, J., *Death, Burial, and Rebirth in the Religions of Antiquity: Religion in the First Christian Centuries.* (Oxon, 1999),

Dermot, H., and Quaglia., L. "European Perspectives on the Global Financial Crisis: Introduction". *JCMS* volume 47, number 5, (London, 2009), 939-953.

Falola, T. *Violence in Nigeria: The Crisis of Religious Politics and Secular Ideology,* (New York, 1998).

Fessy, T. "Bossangoa: Why CAR has descended into violence". Available at: http://www.bbc.co.uk/news/world-africa-25354584, Visited:20/12/2013 (13 December 2013).

Frykenberg, R. E., *Oxford History of the Christian Church: Christianity in India: From Beginnings to the Present,* (Oxford, 2008)

Garcia, A., "The Gailygrind: Russian Neo-Nazi Group Kidnaps and Tortures Gay Black South African Student in Latest Attack (Video)". Available at: http://www.thegailygrind.com/author/amgarc11/, visited: 08/11/2013, (2013).

Ghosh, P., *"New Human Species Identified from Kenya Fossils".* Available at: http://www.bbc.co.uk/news/science-environment-19184370, visited: 20/10/2013, (2013).

Glove, G., "Ethiopia: Hollywood Actor Danny Glover Calls for Ban on Landmines". Available at: http://www.irinnews.org/report/52181/ethiopia-hollywood-actor-danny-glover-calls-for-ban-on-landmines, visited: 24/10/2013, (2004).

Görmüş, Ş. and Kabasakal, A., "Are Economic Crises and Government Changes Related? A Descriptive Statistic Analysis". *International Journal of Human and Social Sciences.* Available at: http://www.waset.org/journals/ijhss/v5/v5-13-130.pdf, visited: 08/12/2013, (2010).

Hviding, E. and K. M. Rio, eds, *Made in Oceania: Social Movements, Cultural Heritage, and the State in the Pacific.* UK: Sean Kingston Publishing Herefordshire, (2011).

Jaafar, M. I. E. and Charlie, L. W. M., "Women's Rights in Islam Regarding Marriage and Divorce". *Journal of Law & Practice.* Available at: http://wmlawandpractice.com/2011/04/11/women%E2%80%99s-rights-in-islam-regarding-marriage-and-divorce/, visited: 20/11/2013, (2011).

James, J. *Dishonest Criticism: Being a Chapter of Theology on Equivocation and Doing Evil for a Good Cause,* (Chadetson, 2009).

James, W., *The Varieties of Religious Experience.* USA: Viking Penguin, (1982).

Janz, B. B., "African Philosophy". In C. Boundas (ed.), *Companion to 20th Century Philosophy.* Edinburgh University Press. Available at: http://pegasus.cc.ucf.edu/~janzb/papers/37AfPhil.pdf, visited: 30/11/2013, (2008).

The Journal, "*UK Financial Crisis 'as Serious as a War'*". Available at: http://www.thejournal.co.uk/business/business-news/uk-financial-crisis-as-serious-4399031, visited 04/12/2013, (4 Dec 2009).

Labaton, S. and Zeleny, J., "For Obama, a Chance to Reform the Street Is Fading". *The New York Times,* p. B1. Available at: http://www.nytimes.com/2009/09/15/business/15obama.html?ref=businessspecial4&_r=0, visited: 05/12/2013, (2009).

Lowrey, A. and Popper, N., "World Leaders Press the U.S. on Fiscal Crisis". *The New York Times,* p. A1. Available at: http://www.nytimes.com/2013/10/14/us/warning-of-global-risk-leaders-urge-us-to-solve-its-debt-limit-crisis.html, visited: 05/12/2013, (2013).

Michael M. M., "Why Is There Only One Human Species?" Available at: http://www.bbc.co.uk/news/science-environment-13874671, visited: 1/10/2013, (2011).

Ngunjiri, F. W., *Women's Spiritual Leadership in Africa: Tempered Racials and Critical Servant Leaders.* New York: State University of New York Press, (2010).

O'Shea, J. R., "America Philosophy in the Twentieth Century". Available at: http://www.ucd.ie/philosophy/staff/jamesoshea/oshea/josamerphil.pdf, visited: 02/09/2013, (2000).

Pomfret, R., "2.1. Finance: EUCAM: EU Central Asia Monitoring: Central Asia and the Global Economic Crisis". EUCAM National Series Policy Brief, *Asian: EUCAM Project,* (2009).

Schubert, C., "*Worse Than North Korea in Hollande Makes a Start*" Available at: https://ip-journal.dgap.org/en/ip-journal/topics/hollande-makes-start, visited: 04/12/2013, (2013).

Singer, P., *A Companion to Ethics".* (Oxford, 1993)

Spencer, H., *The Right to Ignore the State.* N.W.: Freedom Press, (1850).

Lagi, M., Bertrand, K. Z., and Bar-Yam, Y., (July 19, 2011; revised August 10, 2011) "The Food Crises and Political Instability in North Africa and the Middle East". Cambridge: New England Complex Systems Institute. Available at: http://arxiv.org/pdf/1108.2455.pdf, visited 10/11/2013.

Theos., (2013) *The Spirit of Things Unseen: Belief in Post-religious Britain.* London: Theos. Available at: http://www.theosthinktank.co.uk/publications/2013/10/17/the-spirit-of-things-unseen-belief-in-post-religious-britain, visited: 10/11/2013.

Trueman, C., "History Learning Site: The Causes of the Vietnam War". Available at: http://www.historylearningsite.co.uk/causes_vietnam_war.htm, visited: 06/11/2013, (2000-2013).

UNICEF., "Children Accused of Witchcraft" / Les Enfants Accusés de Sorcellerie". Available at: http://www.unicef.org/wcaro/documents_publications_5471.html, visited: 30/10/2013, (2011).

Walshe, M. O'C., *Buddhism and Sex*. Available at: http://www.accesstoinsight.org/lib/authors/walshe/wheel225.html, visited: 21/11/2013, (2006).

Zingales, L., "*The Perverse Politics of Financial Crisis*", Project-Syndicate, *Social Europe Journal*. Available at: http://www.social-europe.eu/2011/07/the-perverse-politics-of-financial-crisis/, visited: 08/12/2013, (2011).

www.ingramcontent.com/pod-product-compliance
Lightning Source LLC
Chambersburg PA
CBHW020538290526
45786CB00002B/940